A CONTEMPORARY RENAISSANCE

A CONTEMPORARY RENAISSANCE

Gülen's Philosophy for a Global Revival of Civilization

Sulayman Ashrati

NEW JERSEY • LONDON • FRANKFURT • CAIRO

BLUE DOME

NEW YORK

Published by Blue Dome Press
335 Clifton Avenue, Clifton
New Jersey 07011, USA

www.bluedomepress.com

Library of Congress Cataloging-in-Publication Data Available

ISBN: 978-1-68206-008-7

Printed in Canada

Contents

بسم الله الرحمن الرحيم

In the Name of Allah, the All-Merciful, the All-Compassionate

Foreword

I met Dr. Sulayman Ashrati more than once, heard him speaking and enjoyed his writing about Bediüzzaman Said Nursi, may Allah bestow His Mercy upon him. His interesting style of writing and his incredible ability to dive into the biographies he writes about struck me. I can comfortably say from what I read that he possesses a highly refined aesthetic sense and that his writings have a vivid appeal as if they were masterpieces in an intellectual frame or as if they were intellectual thoughts in an artistic frame. He has the ability to capture subtleties and allusions. He thoroughly looks into the depth of what he is writing about and he has a vast and rich comprehension of the language. He is also rich in knowledge, uses powerful arguments and to him intellectualization is a constructive building procedure; for thoughts are edifices and thinkers are architects while time and place are the substances of construction.

Dr. Ashrati entered Fethullah Gülen's intellectual and spiritual realm. He brought his thoughtful architecture to life in dealing with the man's thoughts. He often pointed to the environment in which Gülen was raised in. Indeed, it was a rich environment in its edifices and architecture that were constructed by the Ottomans' hearts and spirits. They had watered their intellectual masterpieces with the nectar of their art, their gnosis and their spiritual beauty which had a great impact upon the formation of Gülen's thoughts, the construction of his soul and the enriching of his imagination. Each word that he wrote was a brick in his lofty intellectual edifice. Ashrati says, "Mr. Gülen's philosophy was established upon having faith that the work of the intellectual is essentially constructive work." He also says, "Deep faith enables the body to embody the soul and enables the soul, which is the idea, to embody matter. In that sense, the idea transforms into a hand that is able to build, to a back that holds, to spades that dig, workers who accomplish, and organizations that fund and supervise. These are some of the qualifications that Mr. Gülen has. To him, the Qur'an is what lifts up man to bring about an active individual and an awakened society." Any civilization begins with a thought and ends with knowledge and between the beginning and the end there is endeavor, will and determination.

One of the characteristics of Gülen's thought, as seen by Ashrati, is his extraordinary capacity to quickly transform radiant energetic thoughts to edifices of massive organizations in the concrete realm of reality. Because of this unique characteristic, Gülen's thought relied upon cultural transformation, which he himself set the general guidelines for in many of his invaluable books, such as *Kendi Dünyamıza Doğru*[1] (As We Are Building Our Civilization) and *Ruhumuzun Heykelini Dikerken*[2] (As We Are Erecting the Edifice of Our Spirit). In Gülen's opinion, civilizations struggle for one purpose, a desire for self-affirmation. At the same time, this struggle is a strenuous effort that is supported by the spirit of the *ummah*[3] that seeks to maintain its independence from others and its uniqueness.

These cultural and spiritual epiphanies essentially depend on the ability of the Muslim to transform and renew himself and upon his realization of the intellectual dimension of his belonging to a glorious universal system. Gülen stands against all feverish attempts to rob the Muslim of his personality or to blend his individuality. This is why Ashrati affirms, "Gülen represents a golden chain of blessed predecessors who emerged in different eras and places. They devoted themselves to service, to worship and to calling people to Allah. They exhibited benevolence and excellence in serving their *ummah*."

---

[1] This book was also published in Arabic with the title *Wa Nahnu Nabni Hadaratina* (ed.).

[2] This book was also published in Arabic with the title *Wa Nahnu Nuqimu Sarh ar-Ruh*, and in English with the title *The Statue of Our Souls* (ed.).

[3] *Ummah*: the Muslim community throughout the world.

The clamor and nosiness of cultures conceal the human being from himself and drown him in the ocean of his culture which is filled with empty shells. As for the Islamic civilization, as Gülen sees it, it is a civilization that relies on the individual being the essential component of its existence. It sets its goal in leading his soul to ascend to lofty stations of mastery and self-control that brings man in proximity to the Originator of existence.

Any culture that does not facilitate the means by which man can combat his ego to spiritually ascend from the relative to the Absolute and from the limited to the Delimited is an inadequate culture that leads to stumbling and failure. Gülen does not want the authority of this kind of culture to reach the Islamic world.

Dr. Ashrati in analyzing Gülen's thought says, "Because Gülen has a humanitarian perspective and an inviting universal philosophy he set his measuring scale on easing and facilitating that which characterizes the essence of the Islamic creed; for this is its original nature. Whenever the Islamic call deviates from its origin and essential characteristics, the reception of all nations to the religion that Allah intended for mankind is postponed. This is why today's world is not ready to comprehend the requirement of the universal spiritual civilization whose landmarks Gülen illustrates in his writings. This usually happens when we neglect the innate nature of man who has an ever renewing intelligence and who has the capacity to experience and to navigate one phase after another. But when man gathers himself and unifies his essence he becomes very receptive to the requirements of this civilization because these requirements are in harmony with his innate nature which Allah originated him with. In all of his writings, Gülen bets on man and on his fascinating abilities to transform himself from one state to its complete opposite. He bets on man's limitless will which forms the purpose of his existence. This will is mighty and vanquishing and it helps him to transform, to change, to cross obstacles and to alter what he needs. It enables him to overcome hardships and to remove obstacles to reach goals.

As Ashrati says this extraordinary will was displayed in one important achievement towards establishing the work of an intellectual civilization. It was publishing the *Hira* magazine in the Arabic language in Turkey, which was the crowning moment of several difficult phases of endeavor and persistence which many great citizens went through there. They spent their whole lives to achieve this triumph in the battle of restoring spiritual identity and civil relevance. Publishing *Hira* magazine was an indication and an open declaration that a new dawn had risen.

According to Ashrati, the path of civilization, which Gülen illustrated, would never fail in consuming the whole world in its spirit and in its vast intellect. This is because its Source is a Lofty Source. It is Divinely supplied. Thus, its ability to absorb is limitless and its desire to expand and extend is non-stoppable. This civilization widens the field for the self to manifest and to excel itself. Humanity previously entrusted itself to the Islamic civilization for many centuries and today it is ready to do the same if the Islamic civilization would only follow the requirements to assemble this civilization. Islamic civilization does not bargain with man and it does not flatter him to justify his faults or to overlook his failures or to affirm the continuation of his weaknesses. It is as if the secular culture tells him, "Do not worry if you are falling; for you are responding naturally to your animalistic nature." It is a culture that justifies to a large extent the weak and basic desires of man. It does not pay attention to the other powerful aspects which enable him to refine himself and ascend beyond his weaknesses in order to reach a state of mastery which the Islamic civilization enables him to reach.

There is no doubt that we are stepping towards understanding humanity's power even though until now the steps we are taking are slow. Nonetheless, these steps are in the right direction. Ashrati says Gülen has turned our attention towards this power. He explained that it exists within us in the depth of our innermost beings. Without this power, man feels that his life is meaningless and so difficult that he wishes not to exist at all. This causes him to become ill and afraid of existence itself. Gülen turns our attention to that power and points to it, encouraging man to go after it in order to discover it and bring it forth to the visible realm to use it in building his individual strength and to strengthen his culture. This is very important because it is the core of what religion calls for and what Islam invites people to; for Islam is a religion and a civilization which takes that inner power as the foundation upon which it establishes its intellectual edifices and its ethical and civilized principles.

Adib Ibrahim ad-Dabbagh

Chapter One

The Place of Reason in Gülen's Thought

The tree of Islamic ideology has expanded within a natural structure that has a root firmly established. The root consists of the Qur'an and the Sunnah. The tree has eight branches which are the result of the generations of legislation which the scholars of Madinah as well as sociologists and Muslim intellectuals deduced through detecting new daily concerns and by examining values and difficulties to discern what is permissible and what is forbidden.

Civil incidents caused Islamic thinking to go in different directions full of vigor and complexities, but governed by historical conditions, social elements and spiritual and ideological inclinations. These facts earned Islamic ideology its rich identity which is characterized by pluralism. This is because it emerged from a great civilization that flourished for centuries absorbing all branches of universal sciences through synthesizing the polarized aspects of the theoretical and the practical sciences in all civilizations that were either contemporary to the Islamic era or existed before it.

There is no doubt that the universality of the Islamic religion is the foundation of an intellectual opening that is characterized by diligent effort to deduce rulings (*ijtihad*) in Islam. Such diligent research is the offspring of Divine legislation that came to protect all people regardless of their countries and eras. It covers the demands for civil renewal; for within it there is a flexibility that is governed by a cautious spirit to maintain the foundation and standards.

When we speak of Islamic intellect, we mean the dynamic application of the theoretical knowledge which the Islamic intellect pursues in all fields of knowledge through which it achieved and cultivated considerable treasures which formed the heritage of the *ummah* and its credibility upon which its civilization was built and its spirit formed. The Arabic culture was based upon poetry but after Islam came and spread across the continents, it acquired many sciences that were founded by the religion of Islam. The diversity of nations that embraced Islam widened the fields and categories of these sciences and full involvement and participation took place. The result was a rich heritage where humanity reached its pinnacle in all fields at the time. All fields of sciences and arts flourished under the Islamic civilization.

The identity of this Islamic ideology cannot be limited to the range of the original sources, the Qur'an and the Sunnah, for the growth of Islamic thinking was dynamic. It was the result of synthesizing Israeli, Greek, Indian and other cultures. All of these cultures formed a dimension that touched Islamic ideology and were used to strike examples and deduce lessons. We must admit that the identity of Islamic ideology is made up of collective synthesized bricks that form an original wall where plurality is the main pillar upon which the structure is built, as if it were a tree with various branches that has a firmly established trunk expanding its branches and growing its leaves in different directions.

Islamic jurisprudence continued to exercise the mission of examining social matters and civil issues from the perspective of Divine Legislation. Islamic ideology tried to propose maps with the lofty boundaries which Divine law demands and which are in harmony with its main goals which ensure the path of civilization from different ages and places, and in accordance to the changes that life brings.

If we would like to simply define those who energize thought and jurisprudence we can say that thinking is the intellectual activity which is geared towards understanding life and existence by analyzing the realities that are connected to the human being in his past, present and future considering his true humanity, his essence, his individuality and his integration with collective humanity. He has the capacity to transform and to meet challenges that determine his fate. The ultimate goal of this realization is to build a perspective based on direct experience that can govern the social, civil and existential phenomena for the purpose of facilitating some degree of control or security for man during his journey in this world. Thus, to define "jurisprudence" we can say that it is a field of limiting life's mishaps and governing civil and social activities by putting suitable limits that are in conformity with the abiding Divine law.

To be objective in this discussion we have to recognize the place of jurisprudence in the ladder of Islamic research and approaches in the past. It gradually rose towards excellence and loftiness depending on the thinkers. The deterioration of growth in the Islamic civilization has always been synchronized with the slowness of progress in jurisprudence and whenever dogma and superficiality have affected the aspects of life in both the spiritual and physical spheres.

Jurisprudence was always known to be a science. The word "science" was peculiar to legislation. This was because exerting intellectual effort to deduce rulings has always been naturally and closely tied to the Book and the Sunnah; for the main principle was that no one should deduce any ruling unless supported by a scriptural text or by referring to a similar analogy (*qiyas*) or preference (*istihsan*) or other jurisprudent principle.

In the past Islamic eras, the jurist (*al-faqih*) was given a preferred position, and was given the role of issuing religious rulings (*fatwa*) and guiding legislation. Today, we find the intellectual takes a prominent position in spite of the decline in noble morals which we see. This is due to the close relationship between nations and communities with the dominant culture. Moralities have been drowning in the murky sea of policies that promote dissipation and profligacy. Moralities are falling with a media that promotes material consumption and greed.

The surging culture of globalization and the sterile civil weakness in our Islamic societies makes the *ummah*'s soul thirstier for originality and long for a distinctive character. This is due to the *ummah*'s consciousness which is deeply rooted in the principles of its creed, and no matter how it deteriorates under pressure, this conscience will always remain, refusing to fully give up its foundation whether on the cultural level, the level of creeds or on any level from which its true identity sprung.

Today, jurisprudence and ideology form one fountain that waters the guiding foundations which meet the condition of caution, investigate the meaningfulness of the path, the continuation of growth and development, and the making of history.

The intellectual of today's era, the era of bidding on a determined future, comprehends the facts of his time more. He realizes the demands of his place and he has a deeper awareness of the requirements which secure doctrine while guiding the *ummah* to move forward in the right direction.

Today, the intellectual is automatically a philosopher because he is deeply engaged in rational reasoning. At the same time, he is a jurist (*faqih*) because of the demand of exerting his utmost effort to answer legislative questions in light of Divine guidance. He is also a strategic expert because he is aware of the extending dimension which ties him to the future but also to the ultimate goal.

When we speak about an intellectual like Fethullah Gülen, we are speaking of a discretionary contemporary intellectual who became qualified for this role by his path of toil which attracts attention and stimulates further effort with its piercing efficiency, comprehensive goals, applicable methods and a historical testimony of its validity.

The Epistemology of an Intellectual Movement

There is no doubt that for every thought energizer there must be a goal to pursue, a function to perform, a particular problem to investigate, or rationale either practical or theoretical to contemplate. Contemplating the absolute or the subjective must satisfy within one an internal desire, or dissolve a particular confusion, or substitute the fluidity of the living reality with a theoretical reality which the mind is inclined to visit to form a rational argument, or to find an explanation for one of the persistent motivations.

Even though, philosophical thoughts are diverse and are divided into many branches, there are two main schools of thought that persist in

drawing the intellectuals' attention due to their applicable characteristics which suits the nature of the self with its essence and its selfish
inclination that seeks self-benefit. These two schools of thought are the
pragmatic and the dogmatic ideologies.

The pragmatic ideology is similar to the dogmatic ideology in how
they both focus on using skillful conjecture and their promoters are
deceived by emotional excitement in mobilizing rebuttals, and being
intoxicated by a temporary and perishable success in defeating their
opponents. Arrogance prevents them from seeking true insight into
the consequences of the ideologies they are promoting. Such ideologies
produce policies and doctrines that are the natural products of franti-
cally excited perspectives that are characterized by reckless arrogant
ideas and philosophies that are void of noble moralities which cannot
last. As soon as the leaders' enthusiastic fury comes to an end, boredom
and emptiness settle in and moral looseness spreads leading to a certain fate of spiritual sterility and misery and enthusiasm fades away!

Pragmatism is ruled by the spirit of attaining hasty victory and
looks for personal gains. In the modern era, pragmatism was born out
of Machiavellianism and it did not engage in the political field but it dis-
cussed ethics and universal values. Machiavellianism was the cursed
tree from which a whole forest grew[4] in opposition to logical reasoning
and common sense.[5]

In comparison, dogmatism blindly drifts after a ready-made idea
and a drawn line that claims to follow a belief in the supernatural. It tends

---

[4] Machiavelli justifies his philosophy, which promotes instrumentality (meaning the
    ends justify the means) as a pragmatic perspective that can be concluded when one
    contemplates the reality of humanity and the selfish nature with which the human
    being is born. This conviction produced many other philosophies of materialism
    and sensuality such as the evolution theory or Darwinism which is based upon the
    concept of the survival of the fittest. All of these philosophies which branched out
    from the evolution theory deny the Divine presence and declare the death of God.
    Its grandchild, Freud's theory followed the main principle and reduced activity to
    sexual desires. According to this theory, it is the libido which leads to doing good
    or to creativity or to doing evil or to destruction.
[5] Common sense is a literal translation of the French phrase "le bon sense" and it is
    equivalent to the Arabic word "al-muru'ah."

to empty the intellect of its dynamic research. It obstructs it from the truth in the way it evaluates and makes choices. When the mind is trapped in association with dogmatism it finds itself in the position of blind surrender, waiting to receive external authoritarian instructions.

There is motive behind dogmatism which is to defend its axiom that is taken to be the absolute truth. Thus, dogmatic thoughts emerge as a reaction to what threatens the validity of its axioms. It takes the form of: "I do not see except that which the pharaoh, who acts as Lord, sees." Nonetheless, the pharaoh decides what his will, his opinion and his ego demands. In this way, life enters a vicious circle. There is no originality, no renewal and no responsibility, but there is rather deterioration, passivity and a death like state.

Under the shade of dogmatism, there is a higher source to energize and assemble which the dogmatists raised to a holy station. He follows the instructions of the pharaoh which has a perishable nature; for there is no prospect of renewal in front of it. The one engaged in dogmatism executes the instructions literally by any means that are habitually followed.[6] When thinking follows a modality it becomes an instrument for calcification; for modalities are hollow and are not a soil that can be fertilized to grow fruit. Dogmatic thoughts adapt perspectives rather than energize the activity of the intellectual faculty or encourage creativity.

While dogmatism means full surrender to authoritarian commands, be they governmental or philosophical creeds, pragmatism frees itself from moral checks and swiftly transgresses its liberating claim and declares, "Let him work, let him pass." This transforms it to a blind instrument of taking advantage of others; for its goal is utilitarianism and it seems to achieve it by any means possible. In pragmatism the logic of living is based upon possessing and seizing which led to capitalism which resulted in brutality. Capitalism reached the extent of random bidding for material gain that left societies prey to its ferocity.

---

[6] Islamic jurisprudence (*fiqh*) prohibits imitations in matter of worship and does not allow it except for the simple-minded who cannot pursue the means to illumination.

Faith-Based Reasoning

Along with pragmatism and dogmatism, there is a third ideology which is the faith-based ideology. Faith (*iman*) demands certitude (*yaqin*). In other words, it demands believing in the transcendent reality not in the current visible authority. It also demands taking responsibility and being committed to the truth. Faith means being willingly engaged and devoted to harmony without seeking material or selfish gain, only wishing to be rewarded by Allah.

Faith-based ideology essentially requires following what one believes in like a river that is never cut off from its source. The danger of having "to follow" what one believes in occurs when the mind is locked on the outer picture within the set-boundaries made by other men who may have exerted reasonable intellectual effort to draw these boundaries. This causes the faith-based ideology to become closed and passive; for it relies only on the inheritance of ancestors as it follows their traces without finding a way out of the emotional level of attachment and transcending it to the level of understanding and verification through direct experience.

Most of our relationship with our history follows that pattern of closed thought. Our relationship with our heritage does not go beyond admiring it and taking pride in its achievements, but it is void of the aspects of deep examination, true understanding and applying this understanding. Thus, our connection with our heritage rendered a negative effect void of any beneficial fruit. It became mere claims, a way of manipulation and covering up the truth that comes from ignorance. We are like the one who is occupied with how to sell his official uniform and get his share of the price!

Nonetheless, faith-based ideology can become open, effective and dynamic when it comprehends not only the *ummah*'s rich spiritual and intellectual heritage but also the collective heritage of the philosophies and history of humanity as a whole. It must comprehend the paths of different religions and civil movements and how they affected the state of people. It must become able to contain the different stages and the consecutive historical roles in order to feed its intellectual process and digest that history to produce a spirited perspective that moves towards strengthening the true identity by expanding its capacity and readiness.

An opened faith-based ideology is not limited to the cultivation of what the mind acquires from positive interaction with cultural and universal knowledge, but it is able to gain the capacity to adapt its force to digest all of these thoughts, and so finds its origin and integrates it into its field of knowledge in order to expand the ground of its originality with its diverse branches. This arms the spirit with the ability to make intellectual deductions which allows the formation of sound perspective. This liberates the intellect and restores its dynamic engines that were dormant or dysfunctional as a result of severe deterioration and chronic stagnation of its role in civilization.

Gülen's Intellectual Philosophy

Gülen's call for having an honest look at life, at reality as is, and at civility strengthens his faith-based ideology and utterly cuts it off from the tattered ideologies that settled in the Muslim world due to the tendency of resignation which established an abysmal gap between Muslims and life. This way of thinking led them to deviate from their role in constructing life on earth and led them to surrender to a passive spirit that is alien to Islam.

The duty of inviting people to Allah, in Gülen's thought, must stem from a real objective and ever renewing perspective. It must adapt to intellectual modernization and to the gains of scientific developments and the pedagogical interaction with contemporary nations. This is why it depends on spreading on earth and introducing Islam to others through providing several forms of aid, investment and physical presence. After all providing help and developing material advancement is one of the aspects of Islamic values. When these values are fully embraced and actualized, their excellent benevolent[7] effects manifest on earth in a tangible way that people benefit from. Thus, they fall in ardent love with Islam and become an integrated part of its geography!

---

[7] In the Islamic perspective, excellent benevolence (*al-ihsan*) means attaining the ideal station in behavior, in action and in embodying the creed's spirit.

This faith-based ideology is inspired by the Prophet's life. The Messenger of Allah, peace and blessings be upon him, continued to strive to establish a constructive creed until his last breath. His goal was to firmly establish man's place on earth and to strengthen humanity's special position. This is expressed in his saying, "If the end of the world came to one of you while he has a seedling in his hand which he was about to plant, let him plant it!"[8] The pursuit of continuous renewal is expressed in Allah's saying, *"Indeed, Allah does not change what has afflicted a community unless they change what is within themselves"* (ar-Ra'ad 13:12). This is a philosophy of living which is emphasized in several positions in the Qur'an where Allah often repeats, *"those who have faith and do pious deeds."*

Thus, Gülen's thought is in conformity with the Divine law that is prescribed for man and which confirms his responsibility in this world. It is a thought that is liberated from a problematic point of "pre-destiny and free choice" which often occupied the minds of our ancestors, confused them and made them think in a vicious circle.

Gülen affirmed the perspective of taking responsibility, which not only leaves room for free choice concerning one's actions and choices, but it also affirms man's role in writing the history of this universe as Allah's vicegerent on earth. Gülen expressed this by saying, "It is possible to carry on the role of vicegerency, which Allah gave to the human being, on the basis of the right He gave him to intervene to some extent in all aspects of existence and events."[9]

With the arrival of Islam, the frame of universal ethical responsibilities, being truthful, which Muslims were charged with, were determined. Islam demands Muslims to be the most benevolent people on earth and follow what is known to common sense or our innate nature and prohibits that which is detestable to our innate nature. By comprehending this duty which the Divine law demands of man, Gülen constructs his perspective of the future by establishing a comprehensive

---

[8]   Narrated by Imam Ahmad in his *Musnad* (Reference), p. 3109.

[9]   Gülen, *Adwa'u Qur'aniyyah fi Sama' al-Wijdan* (Qur'anic Lights in the Heavens of Conscience), p. 43.

ideology and founding a vision towards a renaissance where leadership is given back to a nation that is qualified by its essential universal creed to become the wise judge and the spiritual leader of all the world.

To Gülen, the faith-based ideology is not a movement to control and is not a theoretical activity. It is not an immersion into an absolute metaphysical dimension that is cut off from life. On the contrary, to him this faith-based ideology is an applicable term and a civilized comprehensive plan that visualizes a better future for humanity. To him thought and action are two faces of one coin and are the foundation for a renaissance. His philosophy stems from recruiting the spirit that is rooted in the principal of Divine law; for the first goal is to construct the characteristic of a free human being who takes responsibility for his actions. Through constructing the individual, a community can be constructed which can bring honor back to man and back to the true spirit of Islam. This can open for humanity new horizons of understanding and cooperation considering we are all Allah's servants.

In Gülen's thought to be qualified as the most benevolent *ummah* is not without conditions and requirements and the *ummah* would not be granted this until it qualifies itself with the description given by Allah and until it brings these characteristics to life and they become its very nature. This means that being the most benevolent nation is conditioned by qualifying itself in order to truly deserve this title. There is no goodness in a nation that falls short of rising up to this honored position by carrying out our sacred duty in the universe and in the world. This shows that the honor depends not upon theoretical identity but on real application. It depends on executing a program for renaissance and making plans for social problems especially in this current era. Thus, to become the most benevolent nation means to practically embody the qualities of "benevolence and goodness" which Allah prescribed for the Islamic *ummah*. This is why Gülen's thought has always been associated with providing social services along with calling people to Allah. He made social service a manifestation of having pure faith and as a customary aspect of affirming certitude.

In conclusion, Gülen's thought is characterized by presence and faith and its credibility relies on being effective in a living reality by widening the scope of doing good and by making a difference to humans through embracing and applying this faith-based ideology.

According to Gülen, the true intellectual is not one who is overtaken by incoming currents or who gets lost in sterile hypotheses that are cut off from reality and cannot see the degeneration in the present era and so cannot find the remedies. The true intellectual is one who forms a thought in harmony with religion and is based on faith. He must arm himself with a perspective that serves humanity. Without doubt, this person would see the fruit of his efforts no matter how crooked the path becomes. The responsibility an intellectual has towards humanity must not only be that he takes theoretical positions or uses empty slogans on special occasions as mere propaganda. The responsibility of the intellectual is a concept based on action and on exerting his utmost effort to benefit communities and humanity as a whole. Any thought can be rendered fruitless if it does not achieve something that causes it to mature. It has to have its applicable aspect to make the theoretical assumption something believable and want to be chosen because of its achievability when put into action.[10] On the other hand, there is no significance or importance to the fluid thought that cannot be embodied in real life and which does not move the society to develop into what is better.

Religion and the Danger of Falling into Dogmatism

Religion can turn into dogmatism when its principles and values fall into intolerance, racism, sectarianism, isolationism and political alienation. No religion can be safe from the invasion of dogmatism unless there is clarity in its instruction and it is able to transcend to horizons that can make its principles real values concerning their benefit to all of humanity. It must call for brotherhood, cooperation and abandon that which causes corruption.

---

[10] This is close to Gülen's perspective for the practical path which an active intellectual should engage in when he is moving from the level of the mind to the level of utility.

A religion that does not spread its wings to embrace all of humanity and that does not look at humanity as one species that has one Lord, one origin and one ultimate destination is a nationalist religion that is exclusive and reclusive and as such it is the perfect version of dogmatism. This is because the system of principles that limits its field to a particular nation or society becomes a mere ideology or a vessel for an ideology that is incomplete; for one of its top priorities becomes emphasizing nationalism which results in claiming superiority to others and creates separation and an arrogant culture that takes pride in its ethnicity. Most of the nationalistic ideologies are based on such dogmatism which leads its adherents to have double standards. In this way it extracts man's spirit from its humane aspect and replaces it with a reckless attribute that disparages the holiness of humanity that was originally honored.[11]

The concepts of brotherhood have regressed as a result of giving preference to certain ideologies that govern the relationships between people. These ideologies oppose the concept of equality which is demanded by the spirit of humanity. Many contradictions and deviations resulted from applying these ideologies which destroyed the aspects of interconnectedness and cooperation which all religions call for.[12]

A creed that glorifies a race, an ethnicity or a nationality over humanity and over humaneness is indeed a creed that has deviated from Allah, the Lord of the Worlds. It is a creed that plants seeds of hostility between nations. This creed blocks the Path to Allah.

There are two pathways taken by the heavenly religion and the ideological religion. The former considers the whole of humanity and all creatures; for faith has a lordly caring quality that includes all the worlds in its mercy. As for the latter, it is considerate of a nation, a race or an

---

[11] *"And indeed We have honored the children of Adam"* (al-Isra 17:70).

[12] Mr. Gülen says in his comparison between Islam and other religions, "Regarding the religion of the truth, it brought that which is good and responds to the human being's needs; considering that the human being was created for eternity. Thus, sound reason and clear thinking affirm the fact that this religion cannot be ignored or neglected; for this religion meets the human being's desires, wishes and needs." See *Wa Nahnu Nabni Hadaratina* (As We Are Building Our Civilization), p. 177.

ethnicity. This dwarfs the meaning of lordship; for it makes the lord only for a certain ethnicity excluding all others. It creates a lord who abandons what it supposed he created with his own hands.

Religion is a spiritual and ethical reformer. Like a mother, religion is the first thing the generations open their eyes to, grow under its instructions, and adopt its rules within their nature. Having these qualities,[13] religion establishes the main constituents which direct the human being regardless of his relation with the creed; for even if he continues to be ungrateful to the creed, he would still continue to carry the traces of that creed unconsciously because he was raised in its culture and grew up in its environment. This is because religion has its spiritual and ethical effect on the self and somehow it opens an early inner dialogue within the self, especially if he is sentimentally ready. He would always adhere to the rules and adjust himself to its foundations. This makes him the ideal religious person because he is immersed in it and inspired by it even though he may not have an awakened insight that can strengthen his relation with life and with the purpose of his existence and what is beyond it.

Because there are many religions in the world that play an effective role in forming values and measurements, then naturally we can find among these religions some that were preserved in their literal ways. They were sent just as true Islam, which met the conditions that prove it was fully preserved. At the same time, we can find some religions that were altered and deviated and some of their texts show that they were forged.[14]

Between Religion and Ideology

How can a political ideology be distinguished from the religion of truth? Does a religious person actually follow an ideology?

We explained before that an ideology is characterized by a set of customs that are particular to a certain ethnicity, nation or intellectu-

---

[13]   Language and culture also affect the spiritual and intellectual being of the individual.

[14]   As an example read the chapter of Jeremiah in the Bible. You find that Prophet Jeremiah criticized a group of Jews who altered the Torah.

al philosophy. On the other hand, the religion of the truth is inclusively spiritual and so it transcends particularities. It is open to that which is universal and it is humane in its nature and intellectual efforts. Thus, the person who follows the religion of the truth is an individual whose humanitarianism is manifested in his spirit, his ethics and his convictions. If he has not attained a level of lofty humanitarianism then his faith is lacking. Thus, we can see how a Muslim should be a humanitarian who puts his humanitarianism into action. This is because his heart loves the entire *ummah*[15] which in the Islamic perspective is inclusive of the multiplicity of nations and communities regardless of their races, ethnicities, colors and languages. Moreover, Islam is inclusive of other religions that affirm the belief in the Oneness of God, The Absolute, The Lord of the worlds. Furthermore, Islam even sympathizes with the idolaters, according to some Islamic schools of thoughts.[16]

Islam is characterized by its universality because it does not limit itself to a particular ethnicity. Islam speaks to the ordinary human being wherever he is, as expressed in Allah's saying, "*O mankind, what has deceived you concerning your Lord, the Generous, Who created you, proportioned you, and balanced you? In whatever form He willed has He assembled you*" (al-Infitar 82:6–8).

According to the Qur'an, anyone who follows the monotheistic creed, which was originated by Abraham, the father of all the Prophets, is qualified to be called "Muslim." The guidance that the last of all the Prophets, Muhammad, peace and blessings be upon him, has provided is for all people and will continue to be so. Islam will continue to be the most inclusive religion that is open to all nations because of its clemency and the genuineness of its rules. This is why inviting people to Islam

---

[15] Translator's note: The word *ummah* in the Arabic language shares the same root of the word "umm" which means "mother" which gives the word *ummah* a wider meaning; referring to the *ummah* as the mother that contains all of humanity who are connected through brotherhood.

[16] These schools of thought see in the one who glorifies an idol, the readiness to have faith in something so in a sense he is apt to accept worshiping Allah, The One God. This school sees that illuminating the path of Islam to the idolaters is the Muslims' responsibility and so they take the blame of falling short of fulfilling that duty rather than seeing the idolater as one who is gone astray.

and conveying its message is one of the duties of the Muslim regardless of his level and one should fulfill this duty wherever and whenever he can. This is not to achieve some gain for one's ethnicity or personal profit or prestige, but rather to do it as a mercy for all the worlds. As Allah says, "*We have not sent you but as mercy for the worlds*" (al-Anbiya 21:107). Even though the one spoken to in this verse (*ayah*) is Prophet Muhammad, peace and blessings be upon him, it becomes the obligation of every one of his followers who exemplifies his creed and reaches the degree of excellent benevolence.

The ideological creed usually adopts an agenda that favors individuals and a closed circle of elite groups. It gives them preference above others. On the other hand, the sacred creed of religion gives priority to the ordinary human being and defines the conditions of his humanitarianism by focusing on two dimensions. The first dimension is establishing his servitude to Allah the Lord of the worlds, which affirms the freedom of the human being and assures that he would not surrender to any other materialistic or emotional force. His strength comes from Allah; for He is the One who brings into existence, the Provider, the Giver of life and the Giver of death. The second dimension is affirming the ultimate final return of man, and that causes him to lead an ethical life, concerning how he deals with the world[17] without causing him to be engulfed in the world or pant after it unless he gets confused and goes astray and thinks of his existence as a game that has no purpose. Faith makes man feel he is a traveler and there is no doubt that he is returning to his home and so he cares to return prosperous.

Indeed, by establishing belief in the Hereafter in man's conscience, it makes him live his life with a sense of responsibility and with a spirit that is aware of its accountability. This occurs when he is certain that his worldly journey is only a preface to eternal life and in a final destination where he receives recompense for the actions he did, be they righteous or not.

It is clear that both religion and any ideology dictate their authority and demand their adherents to follow. This is because the adherent

---

[17] This is the embodiment of the concept "vicegerency on earth" (*khilafah*).

takes it as a reference of how to act and so he becomes the embodiment of its demands. The transcendent principles of religion or an ideology demand from its adherent to surrender and to comply with its limits.

Nonetheless, there is an essential difference between ideology and religion; for the former has a closed ethical circle that prevents one from opening to others. Even if this ideology tries to develop itself towards humanitarianism, it would still be subjected to disassociation because every pursuit that tries to free itself from the original ideology would remain a cause of division between the followers of this ideology. Those who seek to renew it might end up abandoning the original principles upon which the ideology was based or they might end up forming separate small groups that have no effect on the main group and so its destiny remains unknown.

Regarding the true religious creed of Islam, the matter is different. Whether its followers choose to adhere to the literal texts and strictly abide by its orthodox principles or whether they choose to positively expand their understanding of it and exert themselves to find its ease and leniency, the result will always be the same. The core principle of the Islamic creed is humanitarianism and its values are noble values that honor mankind by Allah's decree, Who appointed man as His representative on earth, as he obtains his strength from the Divine Power of his Creator who created everything. The measurement of reward and recompense are applicable equally and logically to all men. The difference between the strict and lenient in Islam is not a dispute regarding servitude to Allah; for the Lord is Lord of the worlds. It is a dispute concerning the degree and the level of abiding by the religious rules not the humanitarian rules. Thus, extremism is not an embodiment of the verse that clearly states, "*To you is your religion and to me is my religion*" (al-Kafirun 109:6).

Contrary to this you find that Judaism emphasizes ethnicity[18] as a condition of being Jewish. This is an example of an ideology not a true religion which causes disorder and deviation from the humanitarian dimension. In this way, ideologies direct people's emotions and focus

---

[18] To be a Jew you must have a Jewish mother.

on ethnic linage, tribal belonging and biased groups. It deadens people's intellects and turns their consciences towards glorifying a collective ego to which they attribute excellent characteristics and claim superiority. On the other hand, the true creed directs the spirit, the heart and the conscience towards glorifying the Creator of all creatures and universes. It plants within the followers a sense of duty that demands respect and compassion for all of His creation while ideology calls for utilitarian religion that seeks to overpower others. This is evident in the secular ideology of globalization.

Mr. Gülen elaborated on the differences that distinguish the Islamic religion from all of the worldly ideologies which we shall demonstrate later. The purpose of the worldly ideologies is utilitarianism. It gives preference to the immediate selfish benefit over the future wellness of all. It gives preference to exclusiveness over inclusiveness. On the other hand, the Qur'anic purpose is futuristic, inclusive and calculated. Acting righteously in this life can grant one happiness in this life and in the next. There is no significance for worldly gains as long as they do not demonstrate one's faith in Allah which results in acting righteously with all creatures. This is because the Muslim's perspective of life is connected to his belief in the unseen, in the Hereafter and in that which transcends this world. Therefore, to the Muslim, existence is continuous and perpetual. Existence starts by living in this lower realm, which is a realm of action, but it ends in the final abode, which is the realm of harvesting. Thus, the Hereafter is a dimension that distinguishes the Qur'anic ideology from worldly ideologies. This is why we find the word "hereafter" frequently repeated in the Qur'an while it is almost absent in the verses of the Old Testament.

Worldly ideologies are after worldly gains and so they measure their success by how much power, wealth, prestige and control of others they achieve on earth. On the contrary, the Qur'anic creed judges success by the reward that can be reaped in the Hereafter without neglecting or ignoring the permissible fortune in the worldly life. When a community deviates from that ideal, it experiences weakness, humiliation and retrogression which we are actually witnessing today. This is because investing in the Hereafter can be achieved by exerting effort in this life. There is no wonder then that the Qur'an always ties faith with acting righteously as expressed in Allah's saying, "*...to those who believe and do righteous deeds*" (al-Baqarah 2:25).

The Qur'an teaches us to have faith in the Lord, the Creator of the universes. He is the Lord that nothing veils Him, nor barrier nor guardian stands between His creatures and Him. Acting righteously means exerting the utmost effort as demanded by the duty of vicegerency. This means that every human being is responsible for his brother and is responsible for the creatures that live on earth. Moreover, he is even responsible for the environment. By carrying this responsibility man deserves the vicegerency on Earth.

The Elements of Gülen's Thought

There are three sources for Mr. Gülen's thought:

1. The Qur'an and the Sunnah and the biographies of the Righteous Predecessors (*as-Salaf as-Salih*) including Sufi sources
2. General principles and contemporary universal knowledge
3. History and the paths taken by different civilizations and the stages of secular societies

It is clear that the first source forms his sentimentality, personality, his spiritual faith and the philosophy of unification. The Qur'an is the assembling book which not only emphasizes the unification of Divinity and confirms its principle, but it also makes it the constant center of its text. Having faith in Allah, The One and Only, firmly establishes within the soul the logical principle of the unity between the realms of the seen and the unseen. If man really appreciates the value of the seen world he would be thankful for it and would invest in it as a way that can essentially lead to the deduction that the One who brought such an integrated universe into existence is Glorious and Perfect. If he believed in the invisible Founder, he would be certain of the Hereafter. He would also gain the spirit of accountability and watch himself. This prepares him in an excellent way to live his humanitarianism in the most refined way of impartiality, care and integrity.

Sufism provides what refines the soul and gives it the ability to foresee the transcendent horizon which the Holy Scriptures spoke of. The Sufi practices enable the soul to know what is beyond the mind's capacity. Thus, Sufism forms the idealistic spiritual framework to embody the principle of unification with its unseen dimension. This is because Sufism, according to the definition from its associates, is navigating the way towards impartiality and spiritual refinement in order to reach purity (*safa*) and completion (*kamal*). Sufism in its core is tied to the spirit of faith and the base for faith is the creed of unification and the affirmation of the Absolute Power of the Creator.

As for the worldly source and the contemporary universal culture, which is characterized by its empirical aspect, it strengthened the aspect of applicability in Mr. Gülen's thought and his perspective of physical data. Nonetheless, Mr. Gülen trained his mind to digest, integrate and synthesize what it collected of worldly knowledge. Then, he reformulated this knowledge based on his faith which allowed him to filter it from all blemishes caused by the pollution of atheism.[19]

Mr. Gülen benefited from the contemporary materialistic culture's practical aspect which distinguishes it. The Muslims' intellect inherited a residue of centuries of lagging behind and preservation that caused a stagnation of thought that isolated it in a closed circle that does not go beyond certain fields of interactions. This cut off the Muslim mind from following the way of practicality, applicability and research. It stopped it from dealing with vital daily problems that have to do with growth, processing and renewal. These characteristics are what distinguish Mr. Gülen's thought which is opened to the two dimensions of contemporary science—the literary and the scientific. This is why his mechanism of thinking is complete, balanced in its insight, and applicable in its orientations.

It is certain that what eased Mr. Gülen's thought and enabled it to synthesize the knowledge and sciences that the contemporary world

---

[19] We can say that experimental approach stops at the level of knowing the certain (*ilm al-yaqin*) and does not pass beyond it to the higher level of epistemology: affirming the truth of the certain (*haqq al-yaqin*) and experiencing the certain (*ayn al-yaqin*) as the gnostics describe them.

offers, is the fact that he had digested well the heritage of the predecessors (*as-salaf*) as well as his firm immersion in the spirit of the Islamic creed both in worship and in philosophy. Add to this his deep understanding of the Qur'an and the Sunnah and how he tuned his findings
with their treasures, both on the intellectual level and on the level of
the ascension of the heart.

The intellectual identity of Mr. Gülen united his spiritual and sentimental with his logical and executive character. This gave him a balanced inclusive identity that sees the whole picture. He does not see
one dimension only, overlooking the other dimensions while evaluating an event or date. It does not halt the process of cultivating reason
and perspective and it does not take contemplative thought away from
its fruitful practical and executive dimensions.

Islamic Heritage and the Originality of the Intellectual Approach

Without doubt, Islamic epistemology depended in its early stage of
development on an intellectual approach which characterized its origin. Nonetheless, Islamic legislation is essentially a spiritual creed that
demands a strong affirmation that is supported by self-evidential proof.[20]
The investigative nature in the field of exegesis (*tafsir*) and hermeneutic methodology and its dependence on evaluating and defining in the
science of hadith are examples of how Islamic ideology was based on
logic and intellectualism even during its formative stages. Indeed, the
tree of knowledge which grew in the soil of the Islamic civilization relies
on reason in its diverse epistemological branches. Narrations and oral
transmissions have been used as a documenting tool in the Islamic culture
beside the clear metaphysical dimension of its epistemological matrix.

Nonetheless, indulging in oral transmission and incautiously becoming dependent on this source resulted in depositions that harmed the
creed itself. It polluted the spirit of faith that is free of confusion. This
is because it opened the door for speculations and illusion which affect-

---

[20] There is no doubt that spiritual realities cannot be proven yet they depend on
sound reason that renders them logically acceptable.

ed the investigative quality and the intellectual approach to issues. This caused many scholars to deviate from sound reasoning to the extent that most of what they cultivated was mere repetitive documentations that have the gates of originality blocked in its face.

On the other hand, Sufism developed in its pursuit to grant Islamic epistemology an ever reviving quality. Nonetheless, it was also polluted by indulging in myth and so it failed to keep that revival of the epistemological quality, especially as it became the main source of values for the general population and the substance of people's tendencies. This pollution washed away most of the intellectual gains of the Islamic ideology which were gained during the first three centuries of its success.

Many mental recovery movements appeared such as that of Ibn Rushd[21] and others. But they looked at ancient Greek philosophy as their resource. Nonetheless, they tried to filter Greek philosophy from the aspects of polytheism and myth that characterized it. The fruitfulness of this interaction was limited and was exclusively meant for the pundits. This was because those pundits did not aim to break out of the cocoon of the ancient philosophy. The Muslim elite pundits considered Aristotelian epistemology to be the top of the epistemological ladder for man.

In this way Islamic ideology came to a halt and its slogan became "It is not possible to come up with anything more original than that." Centuries of intellectual deterioration followed and caused the whole *ummah* to exit the intellectual arena. It remained an absent player from the making of history until Allah stirred some incidents that gave way to the explosion of a new contemporary blessed Islamic renaissance that promises a new awakening to rectify the effects of intellectual deterioration and to plant the land with that which will renew life.

In this framework, Mr. Gülen occupies a special dynamic position which is hastening the slow revival in which our Islamic world has been immersed beginning from the eighth century.

---

[21] In the field of critiquing we should mention Hazim al-Qurtagi.

There is no doubt that the *ummah* did not underestimate the position of intellectual examination. Nonetheless, it found itself having a revealed Book that moved it from a state of perplexity and metaphysical speculations upon which many ancient philosophies were established. The Qur'an answered the questions of man concerning his origin and destination. It clarified to him the origin of his existence, the Power that brought him into being and that moves his worlds and universes. It made the purpose of his existence clear and it is all based on the foundation of faith. In Islam, faith is the direct connection to the metaphysical realm.[22] The foundation of Islamic faith affirms the Divinity of the Self-Subsisting Lord and the belief in a realm of realities that transcends the mind. This includes a belief in the angelic realm, in the initial decree of evil and good and the belief in the Last Day, the Resurrection, the Reckoning and Paradise and Hell, etc. This is why Muslims feel estranged towards philosophy. They consider philosophy a field of dealing with doubt, speculations, uncertainty and perplexities. They formed this view after studying ancient Greek philosophy which is deeply immersed in speculations, idolatry and it attributed divinity to celestial bodies and stars. To the Muslim, sincerity of faith requires an initial negation of existential doubt and the affirmation of slavery to the Creator. It also requires taking the Qur'an and the Sunnah as the main tools of illumination that reveal the major existential visions which man is often ignorant of and longs to know its mysteries and what is beyond it. This is why Muslims did not need to be involved in philosophy, especially in its ancient framework and looked at it doubtfully. They feared its association with idolatry and did not want to indulge in it for they were worried about the confusion it can cause and how it can affect the core creed. This precaution even reached the science of logic and they disputed about it. Some approved of its validity in supporting religion and defended it while others prohibited it as they considered it a doorway to philosophy and a partner in the effect it causes. This is because of its obscure rhetoric which is inclined to form a culture of doubt with the effect of reducing the level of faith. To those

---

22 *"those who have faith in the unseen"* (al-Baqarah 2:3).

scholars, closing the door of logic meant closing the door of doubt and blocking the gaps from which the artistry of mere conjecture can enter.

Abu Hamid al-Ghazali's view of philosophy and logic reveals their forms which were known to Muslim intellectuals in that era (starting from the fourth century). Al-Ghazali ridiculed philosophy and considered it incoherent. Nonetheless, he approved the use of logic and considered it the core of sound reason which can be attained through faith that is supported by certainty.

There is no doubt that the contemporary Islamic renaissance has modified its position towards these sciences. It discarded the old view of exclusion which harmed the progress of knowledge and Islamic gnosis as a result of being overly occupied with only the science of jurisprudence and the obligatory rites. It busied itself with a denouncing attitude. Thus, the renaissance movement worked hard and exerted great effort to assimilate contemporary sciences and reconsider the importance of the position of reason. It did not undervalue religion, but on the contrary it argued against everything that was antagonistic to its teachings.

From this perspective of revival, the contemporary Islamic renaissance started off in an open environment using all available media to spread the new perspective to reach the mind of the *ummah* using reason as a way of taking off again. Mr. Gülen has been playing a very significant role in the renaissance movement. He is almost the only intellectual who joins thought with action. Whenever he delivers a speech, it is an applicable program. His philosophy, as we explained before, is founded upon combining thinking with action. He transformed ideas into actions and made actions embodiments of ideas.

In this way, the Gülen philosophy can be singled out as a philosophy based on reason that stems from the Qur'an and the Sunnah. He also watered that philosophy from the rivers of the pious and he matured it by interacting with modern sciences. Thus, he has had great accomplishments in the field of systematic applicable thought. We will mention some aspects of these accomplishments in this research.

A Reading of Gülen's Thought

In Mr. Gülen's view, the renaissance cannot be achieved without a masterful strategic and scientific plan. This strategy cannot be determined except by a grounded enlightened ideology that has a firm foundation and well established pillars, clearly settled choices, and it completes its constituents so that it can set off in the right direction to achieve specific goals and the purpose it aims for.

No success can be achieved for this strategy if it is not based on sound reason, resolute determination and an insightful plan that has a vision and can predict expectations. In addition, for every creative thought, there must be a reserve of knowledge, values, and regulations that can help it avoid failure and can aid it to cross all obstacles and emergency situations that may occur along the road. What really distinguishes actions and accomplishments are the masterful planning behind them. Any edifice, let it be material or spiritual, cannot be built except on foundations that aim towards perfection and this cannot be born except within the framework of sound reason and disciplined caution. These were some of the principles and dimensions upon which Mr. Gülen's thought is based. But before we elaborate on its manifestations, we should first ask ourselves what "ideology" is.

According to our reading of Mr. Gülen's writings, ideology is the spiritual force which every individual uses for simulating and giving birth to mental facts to evaluate daily life activities to deduce from them rules by which he can manage his daily activities. Thoughts evaluate the present existents and the expectations that are yet to come and prepare a way to adapt to them. Thought is the intellectual activity by which we face life on both its simple levels and in its complex situations which enables us to manage our affairs in a constructive way. Thought is then the efficient tool which allows the individual, through gradual stages in life, to gain mastery over what his experiences prompt him to receive. Through reasoning, the individual earns mastery over his intellectual skills and applicable knowledge which enables him to control his life and social affairs and to direct it in a positive way that brings him contentment.

Because thoughts have many branches and contrasting dynamics, each intellectual response produced from one of the branches is different in its quality and quantity. Thought can travel on narrow paths focusing only on selfish quests and personal benefits such as those that are required by one's family. This is the intellectual activity of most ordinary people in general. Nonetheless, thought can be motivated by collective concerns regarding one's community and the fate of humanity. This intellectual activity is particular to special people, the prominent and unique intellectuals of the community.

Mechanical Thinking and Masterful Thinking

The priority of useful thinking is to overcome challenges. This is because life is a series of hardships as it says in the Qur'an, *"(He) who created death and life to test you (as to) which of you is best"* (al-Mulk 67:2). This is why all pedagogical institutions in all living nations are keen on raising habitual reasoning in their societies in order to enrich the perspective of the individual and the community. This enables the *ummah* to face its challenges and to find solutions to its problems. This is because the intellectual capacity does not mature unless the individual opens up to his environment, drinks the characteristics of his culture and comprehends the principles of his identity.

There is no human being void of intellectual wealth. What distinguishes people from each other is the wealth of their ideas. Thus, you can find a simple naïve person, one of average intelligence and one who has insight with unbalanced intelligence, who has demonstrative ability. It then goes without saying that on the tip of the pyramids are the elites while the wide base contains the simple and ordinary people. The intellectual activity of the simple individual depends on instinctual motives. This is because most of us indulge in daily affairs with a habitual and mechanical attitude. This affects our thinking and brings our intellectual activity into a static state in which life becomes systematic and a mechanical void of renewals and transformations.

Our environment and educational systems affect our intellectual activity. In addition, our professions and culture control our intellectual growth and development. Nonetheless, each individual carries factors that qualify him for intellectual activities in accordance to his readiness and in conformity with the external influences that he encounters. There are bright and talented people who are distinguished by their brilliant thinking and their ability to form a vision. They have efficient insight and reasoning. They are the leaders of the masses without a doubt. They are the extended branch for their societies. They are qualified to lead and are the candidates to deliver guidance because of their unique traits, intellectual capacities and spiritual motivations which better enable them to measure, evaluate, estimate, manage and cultivate positive results.

Intellectual force picks individuals, communities and nations from the emotional misery which comes to them from materialism caused by the regression of life and the relapse of history that results from overwhelming intellectual stagnation and materialistic retention.

There is no doubt that the most prominent factors of this materialistic retention, which prevents development and life, are deviating from the laws of unity, ignoring or neglecting the laws of the universe, and overlooking the spiritual commands; the only cause of gaining an illuminating insight which leads to an authentic way of reconstructing the self and the society.

Thus, the intellectual is forcibly and actively a healer who diagnoses the chronic ills and the progressive aggravating diseases and finds cures for them no matter how many nights it takes and how many sacrifices he offers. We will show how Mr. Gülen focused on his rescue of the renaissance project in the role of the spiritual physician. He emphasized the importance of providing teams of such physicians who can bring the ultimate alertness to their people.

There is a determined pedagogical system that is based upon fundamental foundations, rules and demanding procedures to maintain the execution of comprehensive reconstruction. The renaissance ideology is a comprehensive ideology that covers all levels of civilization with all of its branches. Thus, this ideology must combine healing with construction and must put in its vision the dimension of time. The same skills by which the intellectual produces productive abilities and sieges potentialities, he also adjusts the pace of construction, quickening the pace when that becomes possible and slowing it when that is deemed wiser.

He takes an active position which the particular situation demands and ascends the degrees of embodiment and execution. Thus, he may act to bring about a rectification or issue a condemnation or he rejects it. These are the three degrees which the Prophet, peace and blessings be upon him, attributed to the responsibility of the intellectual. He determined the intellectual's role and his obligations towards correcting the deficiency in the basic principles of the status quo which he encounters. He said, "Whoever sees that which is rejected by sound reasoning let him change it with his hand and if he cannot then let him change it with his tongue and if he cannot then let him change it in his heart and the latter would be the weakest state of faith."[23]

An idea is an implicit conviction. When it is released it becomes a word or speech. The purpose of speech is to have a degree of influence through eloquence and attracting attention. Speech is an effective connective social leverage that causes a change; for what we demonstrate and argue for is what we would like to become.

Thus, when the word is held within, it continues to be attached to the intention because it needs to be filled until it reaches satiety. When it is fully charged it becomes mature and it reaches the level of emersion which takes it from the static state to the active state, transforming it to an out loud cry and an audible voice.

When the idea is transformed to an utterance it becomes an anti-deterioration speech. It permits the desired transformation to happen. Thus, there is an ultimate relation between the reformer and his thought. The force of the reforming ideas drives its strength and dynamics from the personality and the rightness of the intellectual.

The intellectual who sits in his lofty tower[24] practices philosophizing as a hobby or as a luxury avoiding the reality of his time. He believes

---

[23] Reported by Muslim in his *Sahih*, p. 46 and by at-Tirmidhi in his *Sunan*, p. 808 and by Abu Dawud in his *Sunan*, p. 306 and by an-Nasa'i in his *Sunan*, p. 1351 and by Ibn Majah in his *Sunan*, p. 321 and by Ahmad in his *Reference (Musnad)*, p. 2664.

[24] i.e. who is cut off from the current reality and only indulges in pursuing the metaphysical reality

that contemplative activity and reasoning can only be applied on abstract concepts and on pursuing the supernatural. He assumes theories and propositions that are separated from reality. He is like *Don Quixote* in his imaginary battles. This tendency can also be found in art when some artists claim art for the sake of art, (i.e. without purpose).

The thinker in the high tower demonstrates his propositions without connecting them to the society in which he lives and without concern for the ills and mire of life. He produces ideas that cannot enhance the deteriorating conditions or cure the painful disturbances which his community and nation suffer. It is thought that is the product of vain reality that cannot rescue it from its vanity.

On the other hand, the philanthropic reformer interacts with the current situation, having full knowledge and awareness of it. He fully understands the causes of the suffering and the deterioration in his society and by objective interaction he gains positive responses from people. This is the perquisite of actualizing the hopeful transformation.

If we wonder about the secret energy which the reformist thinker treasures and which enables him to affect a change, we would find that it is the idea that is born within the heart set ablaze with longing. Such longing becomes the mobilizing call which has authority over the elites, considering that they are the most ready to comprehend the call. From the elites, the call extends to the rest of the organism, gathering all around the guideline of the path, which is determined by the reformer's program in accordance to the plan of reform.

What the crowd achieves socially and the civil transformation itself is entrusted to the spirit of the reformative idea which stimulates powers and employs groups to work in the repair and construction fields. Thus, in this respect, the idea is the energizing reservoir by which achievements can be accomplished and transformations can be managed. It provides the construction mechanism with the impetus it requires to attain its optimum purpose.

The idea is identified by its possessor, the reformer, so it becomes him as he becomes it. This makes its influence animated on many levels. All the groups that serve the idea find themselves living in a state of natural tangency with the reformer's personality which is transformed in the collective consciousness to a metaphorical person. He becomes like the sun that shines upon all frozen places, spreading its warmness across the horizon. Therefore, ordinary people hold the reformer in high esteem while the true followers transform this esteem into effective actions. Offering sacrifices to execute the reformer's goal and demonstrating sincerity, faith and genuineness becomes the trait that characterizes their services, making it distinct and effective.

This is how the ideas of the intelligent and charismatic reformers spread across many boarders; beyond the limits of their particular environments and geopolitical boundaries. They become universal philanthropic thoughts that become accepted everywhere.

The experimental thought which Mr. Gülen is pursuing today with the acceptance and appreciation it is gaining, even outside the Turkish society is evidence that when a reformer's idea is cultivated from grounded spirituality and social consciousness that is well-founded and has a wider perspective it becomes a priceless philanthropic acquisition wherever its traces or results reach. No wonder we find many educated circles within the Arab and the Islamic world and even outside the Islamic world that are attracted to Mr. Gülen's thought.

Mr. Gülen's philosophy is established on a belief that the reformer's role is a constructive role in its essence and it has to be directed towards reform and renewal. This demands that the intellectual must have enough skills and abilities which are also supported by Divine grants of success. This intellectual, in his experience of serving and changing finds himself as a physician who has to use cauterization. He patiently and with determination examines the location of illness within the self so that he can amputate the sick organ and guarantee healing and restore wellness.

The ultimate goal of the Muslim reformer in the current era is to plant anew the idea of placing the original guiding element of civilization by finding the original cultural guiding tools by which he can remove the negativities and alienation which overwhelm our civil and our social life and surround us from all directions. This negative alienation is manifested in the readiness to accept foreign cultures that occupy the national consciousness without any competitive alternatives. This manifestation shows our blind acceptance of foreign thought without being conscious of its negative ramifications.

The effort of the reform intellectual is manifested in a two-fold mission; to push away the cultural invasion and to restore the original principles. It is a determined battle of challenging the self. It is a gamble on re-actualizing the original modal and restoring the reign of initiative in the race of creativity, originality, excellence and cultural distinction.

To fulfill the prerequisite pillars to qualify for spiritual leadership (*imamah*), the intellectual must deeply immerse himself in stages of union. He must acquire the capabilities that make him a spiritual human being who comprehends reality and gains a vision of the future by estimating the measures needed to combat the deterioration in his culture so that the *ummah* can overcome the stage of weakness and attain a better way of life and a dignified position.

Mr. Gülen illustrated the evolutionary foundation that every reform thinker must emerge from in order to gain spiritual maturity for his projects of reform and so that his nation can achieve prosperity under his banner. Thus, Mr. Gülen put the Qur'an as the foundation and every servant who dreams to serve this nation must use it for his doctrine, his reference, his guide and his inspirational book.

Because the Qur'an is the ultimate authentic and intelligent thought,[25] anyone with sound reason must master the guidance provided in the Holy Book so that the spirit of the Qur'an can become his character. His soul must drink from the Qur'an's nectar; for the Qur'an is the angelic voice that speaks to both humanity and the jinn and directly addresses their feelings.[26] Indeed, the complete teaching of the Qur'an makes its wisdom always fresh; for "It is the Book that has been standing in the face of all storms and hurricanes since it descended on earth. Whenever the Qur'anic voice rises, we feel as if it had just descended now from heaven."[27]

---

[25]   Gülen, *Taranimu Ruh wa Ashjanu Qalb* (The Soul's Hymns and the Heart's Sentiment), p. 15.

[26]   Ibid.

[27]   Ibid.

"It is the Divinely emanated knowledge which is the ultimate termination of the human consciousness."[28]

To be wrapped in Qur'anic verses, widens the field of the intellect, the intuition, and all the faculties of the human being to an extent that does not limit the intellectual vastness or restrict mental and emotional openness. The Qur'an does not isolate you into a narrow ideology or dogmas that oppose philanthropic values or contradict the lofty ethics of love, peace and goodness.

The illuminating provision, which people with a pure core consciousness utilize as a result of their response to the Qur'an, reflects purity upon the spiritual sentimental findings, clear insight upon the heart, and a refined comprehension upon the mind. Whoever truly understands the Qur'an will find vast oceans to be like a drop of water in comparison to the inspiration which his heart receives, and in comparison to the vast intellect by which he is illuminated he will find the sun's light becomes like mere candle light.[29]

The Qur'an is the greatest place of ascension where the soul is prepared for its infinite capabilities of intellectuality and sentimentality. The one navigating the Qur'an swims into marvelous regions that have impressive signs (*ayat*). He moves from astonishment to being stunned and from being stunned to sentimental storms[30] and through these levels he receives the spiritual and the enthusiastic transformation of the individual and he becomes the caller for the truth.

The Qur'an shapes the responsive souls which are ready to be productive. "It attracts the one in quest of its truth and shapes him, renewing his illumination with Divine lights."[31] Those who are on the verge of delving into the Qur'an, "They call on their full feelings, sentiments, and hearts, and the full readiness of their consciences swim in its ocean that has no like and immediately their emotions and thoughts change

---

[28] Ibid., p. 17.
[29] Ibid., p. 19.
[30] Ibid., p. 20
[31] Ibid.

and each of them feels that he has changed to a particular extent and that he lives in another world."[32]

At the time of the Prophet's mission, the Qur'an brought flocks of Companions whose souls were melted and reformed in accordance to heavenly measures. The Qur'an redefined them and by their behavior they embodied its spirit and translated its meanings and metaphors with their actions. They dug a philanthropic passage for humanity in which the light of wisdom, intelligence and dignity shone upon the coldness.[33]

By the favor of Qur'anic teaching, humanity crossed the abyss of foolishness and associating partners to the Truly Real. The work and the theories of the ancient philosophers who were considered the teachers and masters for humanity, such as the first teacher Aristotle and those who followed him, indulged in polytheism and speculations. Then, Allah sent Muhammad, peace and blessings be upon him, to humanity with a message that awakes and radiates light. It liberated man's ideology from its mythology, clarifying that all natural entities are harnessed entities. The Qur'an established the creed of monotheism as the foundation for the whole construction of logic. It taught humanity how to cross the slippery slope of mythology and false speculations. It removed the contamination of polytheism from the mind and allowed the conscience of man to comprehend the enormity of confusion and made it understand the secret of slavery to the Truly Real[34] and taste the benefits of the Oneness and Unity of God (*at-tawhid*).

By the spread of Islamic lights across the horizons, the edifice of ancient mythology fell and the matrix of idolatry was destroyed. There was no more a deity for goodness and a deity for evil, a deity for harm and a deity for love, a deity of intoxication and a deity for fertilization, a deity for drought and a deity for fire or a deity for storm. All of these ideas were speculations which the mind of man invented in his search for spiritual support. But instead of being guided to spiritual maturity

---

[32] Ibid., p. 21
[33] Ibid.
[34] Ibid., p. 20.

he fell into falsehood and did not realize that the multiplicity of deities is a false perspective that no sound intellect can affirm because it is mere speculations and illusions based on mythology.

The Qur'an gives a true perspective of the universe and it clarifies to man his nature and the truth of his existence and it identifies the source of all that exists. "*O mankind, what has deceived you concerning your Lord, the Generous, Who created you, proportioned you, and balanced you? In whatever form He willed has He assembled you*" (al-Infitar 82:6–8).

"*Recite in the Name of your Lord who created—created man from a clinging substance*" (al-Alaq 96:1–2). It turns man from dialectic arguments, the predetermination ideology and blind mechanism to the first cause of all causes that set everything in accordance to a decree: it is the Initiating Divine Will. "*Blessed is He in whose hand is dominion, and He is over all things competent*" (al-Mulk 67:1).

The storms which continue to polish the *ummah*'s knowledge and doctrines in the social, the economic and the natural fields are evident. It is the metaphysical aspect which is absent from our consciousness and which is the foundation to which all matters submit and all arrangements rely. What we witness today concerning the collapse of our economy and the natural disasters that take place are in accordance to the Divine Will that seeks to discipline us after we followed our own minds due to our spiritual aspect which is an essential part of our existence.

The Qur'an not only shook the creed of polytheism on earth but it also established the foundations for constructing a noble individual which is the seed for having a better community. The Messenger's efforts brought forth its fruits during the stages of decline; for the Muslim personality emerged at that time with its full elements of righteousness. The result was a wonderful civilization based on diversity which was the main factor of the spread of Islam and the cause of its sun shining across the horizons in a very short period of time.

As the Qur'an formed the first generation of Companions who became heroes in the intellectual and the spiritual realm,[35] it made them

---

[35] Ibid.

a blessed distinguished society[36] and it will continue to form chains of pious generations who follow its constructive method and compete in giving and achieving noble goals. "Indeed, the degree of perfection which was achieved by the early generations who lived in the illuminating atmosphere of the Qur'an was a miracle in itself. We cannot find the like of this transformation concerning their level of spirituality, intellection and creativity."[37]

Indeed, Islam is entrusted by the spirit and this means by a thought that transforms into action. When the spirit is stimulated and its charge is completed, the thought turns into motion, into accomplishment and change. The Qur'an prepared for the submitter (i.e. the Muslim) and in general to all human beings that which transforms his soul and refines his heart. It turns the attention of the human being to the importance of spiritual maintenance which prepares him to ascend to a faith-based refined level. By blocking the doors of whims and selfish lower desires and by abandoning the bodily demands the soul can devote itself to creative spiritual activity, to beneficial thoughts, and to an ever renewed giving.

By training the self to reduce that which consumes its energy in vain, the soul's burden is lightened allowing it to fly into the metaphysical horizons where the cornerstones of transforming matter to soul and where souls embody matter exist. This can be achieved by being deeply immersed in worship; for worship guides the soul and fashions it in the best mold so it can have the energy necessary for achieving extraordinary goals.

Indeed, deep faith enables the soul to embody matter, or body, and enables the body to embody the soul. In this way, thought can be transformed to a hand that constructs, to a bulldozer that digs, to groups that accomplish goals, and to committees that supervise and sponsor. These were some of the examples shown by Mr. Gülen that prove how the Qur'an plays an uplifting role in creating an active individual and a progressive society.

---

[36] Ibid.
[37] Ibid.

The Place of Reason in Gülen's Perspective

Reason is an intellectual activity that is the foundation of man's actions. Reason may precede the action, accompany it or follow it.[38] It is clothing the self in precaution and in the logic which man's interactions demand in order not to deny the self and to accomplish one's goal in achieving positive interactions. Whatever man thinks of, he dresses it intellectually with his whole being. If intellectual activity has the same genus of real actions, the whole body and will follow to achieve it, but if intellectual activity is only related to mental issues, the mind creates an embodiment for it and brings it into mental existence to some degree. Mr. Gülen points to two types of mental activities which man may indulge in and which control his perspective of life and his relationship with the universe and with existence.

1. Irrational or deaf reasoning: reasoning that emerges from the mind that is separated from or absent from our immediate perception of the unseen (*al-ghayb*)
2. Spacious reasoning: reasoning that emerges from the mind that is connected with the metaphysical dimension

We could argue that Mr. Gülen distinguishes between two colors of intellectual activities or two ways of reasoning: the sense-based reasoning and the spiritually-based reasoning. The former is closed upon itself and concerned only with matter while neglecting the soul. The latter is connected to matter but concerned with the soul, believing in that which is absent from our immediate perception, the unseen. He sees the visible realm as the extension of the metaphysical realm and that the world is the preparation for the next world.

By illuminating the active intellect, civilizations emerge and life is renewed. This is because constructive thinking pursues attainable possibilities and brings about beneficial ends. Out of the field of possibilities, it brings that which is applicable and useful because it relies on realistic and strategic thinking. It directs the attention and the will

---

[38] Thinking accompanies actions even in the subconscious where the action becomes natural habit. Thinking is the natural course of evaluation after performing an action. Thinking becomes an illuminating vision towards a future action or goal.

to reveal to us how to accomplish the most complex projects and the most difficult chances and the most imaginative ideal goals.

The active intellect assigns the construction of man as the priority, especially concerning the refinement of the soul. Man is the first and the last actor pursuing the goals by which the whole civilization can be refined and by which construction can expand.

Thought has a natural developing aspect; for it too plants the seed and waits to cultivate its fruits. If thought is polluted with fantasy and illusion, which is the metaphysical imagination that is separated from reality, it drowns the mind, makes it sterile and leads it to the worst fate. Sterile thought leads to looseness which in turn leads to the death of civilization. The *ummah* was swept away by sterile thinking which overtook it after the fourth century. This sterile thinking plowed away the *ummah*'s luminous achievements and caused it to enter a stage of division and fanatic quarrels which depleted its material and spiritual resources. Add to that, the role the story tellers of the mosques played in calling people for dull asceticism that demonizes and trivializes life. This encouraged a spirit of lethargy which marginalized the *ummah* and made it content with being on the outer contours of life.

On the other hand, we find that constructive thought is an essential driving force; for it sheds insight into the *ummah*'s capabilities and possibilities. It opens fields of work and renewal for man that makes the meadows of intellectual activities always fresh and flowing as long as they are watered from the ever flowing river of Divine law which burns ignorance to ashes and removes any aimless vanity.

The *ummah* has been asleep for so long and it suffered nightmares of passivity, hesitation and defeat. The *ummah*'s first failure was due to its division concerning its creed where each group accused the other of heresy. They threw away the essential unifying aspect upon which the whole Divine law is founded: "*And hold firmly to the rope of Allah all together and do not become divided. And remember the favor of Allah upon you—when you were enemies and He brought your hearts together and you became, by His favor, brothers. And you were on the edge of a pit of the Fire, and He saved you from it. Thus does Allah make clear to you His verses so that you may be guided*" (Al Imran 3:103).

The Prophetic approach exhibited a role model and we must follow the Prophet's Way (Sunnah) in gathering and correlating. Spiritual deterioration, doctrinal fanaticism and short sightedness spread widely on all levels and transformed unity into fragmentation, strength into weakness, and gathering into dispersing. This caused an intellectual void that took the *ummah* to an abyss until it went astray in a confusing period of accusations of heresy and blasphemy.

In this way, the *ummah* was defeated under the pains of poverty, illiteracy and epidemics. This is because the mesmerizing confusion (*fitna*) brings the wheel of growth to a halt, ruins what was cultivated before and turns the earth into an arid land that cannot produce except what is thorny and bitter. Thus, foreign enemy forces invaded the *ummah* and occupied the homes. The masters of yesterday were defeated and sank to the lowest humiliating level, forcibly paying their tribute as they were sold out. Such are the milestones of the path of decline as it was recorded by the history of this nation.[39]

Considering a heritage full of devolutions and setbacks, contemporary Islamic ideology is rising at the hands of men charged with the duty of spiritual leadership as they take their turn to become the civil and spiritual guardians of the *ummah*. They have immersed themselves in the pursuit of reviving a happier tomorrow in which every aspect returns to its right place. These spiritual leaders comprehended the lessons and took heed of the deterring admonishment. They are prepared to pursue what they strive for by putting their faith and trust in Allah, and realizing that their nation is the one which Allah charged to accomplish what is good and noble. Their eternal motto is: "*You are the best nation produced (as an example) for mankind. You enjoin what is right and forbid what is wrong and believe in Allah*" (Al Imran 3:110).

Without doubt, the head of the spiritual leaders is Mr. Gülen who is like a lighthouse that radiates hope and certainty in prosperity. He

---

[39] Gülen, *Wa Nahnu Nuqimu Sarh ar-Ruh* (As We Are Erecting the Edifice of Our Spirit).

emits a light that demands high esteem and to which wills and men surrender. His fine biography shows evidence of devotion and spiritual richness. His projects and awakening programs show evidence of spiritual maturity and inclusiveness which is bringing fruitful results.

What characterizes Gülen's thought is its continual giving which allowed it to establish the pillars of renaissance. Because of its Qur'anic spirit, his ideology is able to guide, to recruit and to challenge. He derived from the tolerant Islamic law the basics and the foundations that qualify any nation, without any competition, to establish a spiritually mature civilization. This is because Islamic law can guide civilization and expand its physical and spiritual formation leading it towards the service of humanity. It is an idea that is established upon God consciousness (*taqwa*) which does not discriminate between races or ethnicities but pursues what is good and pious for the whole world.

Just as Islamic ideology has proven itself in the past it will prove its genius in constructing life in the future in a way that achieves prosperity that does not diminish or decline as long as man modifies his way in accordance to the Divine Way, holding tight to the most trustworthy handhold. This is because civilizations are established upon balanced thinking which is based upon the two pillars of the soul and the body. Any civilization void of spirituality has no sense of universal compassion and that leads man astray. He would be held prisoner in that which is immediate and corporeal. This causes his expansion and civil pursuits to decline. Virtuous life is a life in which gratefulness is joined with conscience and reason. Without that, societies regress into bestiality that know no values.

This is why the human being must make the construction of his ideology as his first priority and goal in life in order to make his faith complete. There is no true faith without reflection, contemplation and understanding. Sound reason is the result of merging the two pillars of humanity: the worldly pillar and the spiritual pillar of the final abode. Allah created man in order to know and adore Him and to fill the earth and the universe with constructive actions (as the Divine vicegerent) that affirms His worth of praise and to widen the aspects of praise. Thus, pious actions are the essence of worship; for it is the hearts gratification. On the other hand, passive asceticism is turning one's back on one's duties and obligations and this is prohibited in the Divine law because it deviates from the spiritual creed which is emphasized in the Qur'an of the importance of joining faith with pious actions as the basis that leads to attaining the ideal of completion and surrender to the Divine Will.[40]

Similarly, society like the individual must construct its ideology and refine it. This demands that societies care for both aspects: the physical and the spiritual or the worldly and the ultimate so that its path to fill the earth with constructive actions, which Allah demands of us, would not be disrupted. This is because filling the earth with constructive actions is the practical aspect of worship, (i.e. adoring and knowing Allah).

The Aim of Gülen's Goals and Objectives

The construction of the Muslim personality is the ultimate goal of the living pedagogical system which Mr. Gülen follows. This is because by man's efforts, hands and reason, the status quo can be changed to a better state under the condition of having sound reason, spiritually mature vision, and balanced estimations.

Humanity has established many civilizations while being ignorant of the true faith-based way. Man has always sought worship from his common sense and his attraction towards that which is loftier following his innate spiritual nature. He traveled along many paths and pursued many rituals without affirming the Divinity of the Sole Creator, the Lord of all worlds. He was pushed towards worship by his Divinely constructed innate nature, which yearns towards that which is most perfect, complete and the loftiest. Without doubt, the tendency to be inclined towards beauty is Divinely deposited within man. This is the particular characteristic which distinguishes the human being from the rest of the creatures. Allah brought his creation to the highest point by depositing within man a breath of His own Spirit. By this spiritual

---

[40] The Qur'an makes "those who faithfully believe and do pious actions" its motto and the cornerstone of the Holy Book.

breath man has been confused and guided and by It he can accomplish many impressive achievements. The human being is the only creature capable of constructive actions and creativity. This is because Allah assured man's readiness for this by granting him an innate nature that is capable of acting righteously. Allah made the human being the most refined creature for which heavenly guidance is given through the pure chosen ones: the Prophets and the Messengers who guided humanity to that which showed them the path of balance and equity.

Surely, what the human being has accomplished in the eras before the heavenly apostleship disappeared and only its traces remained as testimony for those who can reflect. The cause of the destruction of their civilizations is not due to the passing of time which degenerates everything new and makes old everything that has taken place. The cause of destruction lies in their deviation from the truth and from their sound innate nature. This is what has caused many civilizations to diminish and be ruined until they are completely annihilated. This is what the Qur'an informs us about.

Thus, we must realize, based on what these nations recorded, that their civilizations were not established upon heavenly guidance or upon a message that was Divinely sent down to a Prophet or Messenger and how this caused their annihilation. When any civilization deviates from the Truly Real, the law of the ultimate reality applies to it. This is a simple explanation, but it is the essence of the truth which history testifies to.

The living historical testimony can be seen in the example of the children of Israel. Allah sent down to them countless Prophets and Messengers directing them towards the right creed of the Truly Real. It led them gradually from a barren life to a constructive life so they were able to establish civilized kingdoms. But when their path led them to fragmentation, they were dispersed across the earth and their cities and traces were annihilated as if they were erased from the face of the land they once had inhabited and constructed. The secret cause of this annihilation was their deviation from the heavenly teachings which the Jewish society wants to restore. This deviation led them to face the same fate which many nations that let go of their duty towards Allah faced. Nonetheless, because there have always been some Jews who kept their covenant with Allah, their ethnic group continued to survive and Allah granted that Judaism continue to exist on earth.

All heavenly messages, and in the forefront of all messages is the final message of Islam, cared to inform man of the conditions for civil stability and for establishing a continuous civilization. This is not by promising to establish Allah's Kingdom on earth but by informing man of the factors that can guarantee the continuation of civility. These can be summarized as performing pious actions that are based on the natural innate Divine law (*ash-sharia al-hanif*). They lead to positive construction in the universe by diving into the field of planting pure goodness and by walking forward with faith until the Last Hour is established and Allah inherits the earth and its inhabitants. At this point, man stands for reckoning in front of His Lord and he faces either everlasting bliss or eternal suffering.

Abandoning faith in heaven as a creed does not stop man from constructing the material world and achieving physical gains but the ultimate fate of this materialism lies in being deceived by it. It leads to a disastrous fate that causes utter ruin. This is the path taken by our contemporary civilization which takes pride in its advanced technology and sciences. Its horrible fate can be seen by any who sees. Materialism is leading all of humanity to a horrible fate in spite of the remaining bridges that still connect some societies in the developed world with religion. Danger is coming because the number of people who reject the Truly Real is more than those who have faith. This will ultimately lead to the widening of the gap between the abandoned path of spiritual maturity and the path of confusion which the non-spiritual civilization is taking.[41] This can cause these civilizations to completely stray from

---

[41] This is because abandoning spirituality can take the ethical aspect away from the interacting nations while Divine teaching grants the co-existence of everyone. Capitalism is based on the pursuit of material gain which does not mind taking advantage of others and forcing them to serve the capitalists. In this way, humanity finds itself dragged into wars and confrontational struggles. Capitalist nations compete to dominate in order to have the maximum materialistic gain and this causes conflicts between them which may lead to the destruction of humanity.

the Truly Real and collapse when receiving the same fate of destruction that many nations faced before.

It is important to believe in the One Creator and follow His guidance which guarantees the continuation of spiritual wellness and the condition for attaining tranquility and stability. It also secures his civility and the continuation of a life Divinely secured in tranquility from which humanity would not suffer any misery.

As long as man repels and rejects the truth, dragged down by monstrous materialism, he becomes heedless by indulging in its fleeting pleasures which leads to the decline of his prosperity. There is no fate awaiting vanity except ruin. It is the attitude of time; to drag its tail and surround what the tyrants built crossing their high walls and reaching them.

The Islamic civilization is in its second millennium and it has passed stages of decline and atrophy but it has been coming back as dawn emerges through the darkness. It has become as thin as a thread of hair but it has not been completely cut. This is because it is a civilization that was established upon the pillar of having faith in Allah. This enables it to become well because the spiritual path continues to be good. Nonetheless, it is disturbed by the disturbance of the creed and by the diminishing of its light within the hearts of people. However, Allah wrote that the community of Islam is eternal and everlasting.[42] This is because it is the community within which the Divine Spirit was originally immersed, because it is the final message and the seal of all messages. This means that the Divine law, which Allah is content with, cannot be divorced from it. It is the Divine Authority which demands that we be the guiding ones!

We are the carriers of the revelation and the cultivators of excellence and benevolence by the honor which Allah bestowed upon us to convey the purest of His messages to the earth and to all the worlds. Our Qur'an-based civilization does not change; for it has been preserved in

---

[42] In this way, Mr. Gülen explained Allah's saying, "*Indeed, We have sent down the Reminder and indeed We shall preserve It*" (al-Hijr 15:9).

accordance to the Divine proclamation, "*Indeed, We had sent down the Reminder and indeed, We shall preserve It*" (al-Hijr 15:9).

The Sacred Heritage

Having faith in Allah, as Mr. Gülen sees it, is the cornerstone in constructing renaissances and maintaining civilizations. The role of the leaders is essential in preparing people and leading them forward towards becoming wakeful and acting accordingly. No individual can be qualified for leadership unless he has some successful stock in the market of faith and in having fear of Allah.

To deduce lessons, Mr. Gülen continued to study the record of all successes in the history of Turkey, which had remarkable traces of success. Mr. Gülen studied the history of Turkey and realized that its successes were always achieved at the hands of extraordinary leaders who were steeped in the religion of innate nature and in its purification crucible. In other words, their sincere worship had purified them and dissolved them in the pure crucible. Their rank in spiritual transformation was lofty and it drove them to hold the flag of leadership and to achieve an honorable position for themselves and their nation. Being raised in religious families played a prominent role in making them emerge as remarkable geniuses. Their actions refined their intellectual and constructive efforts to lofty levels. Each of them influenced the collective identity of the *ummah* and each of them is an edifice of the *ummah*'s conscience and a diamond in its great heritage.

The influence of being raised in an Islamic atmosphere had an impact upon polishing the souls of those leaders; for it sealed their doctrine with an engraved seal. The water of faith simmered within the depths of their beings, causing the lofty traits to overwhelm their beings and strengthen their habitual rejection of falsehood. It defined their intellectual activity and reasoning and empowered their receptivity to the Divine Decrees and refined their determination to be productive. Thus, they became strategic planners of the first class.

The greatest fortune that life and history can give to people and nations is to appoint a genuine pious leader to lead them through all stages of advancement and who is able to deliver. Surely, the power of the individual, no matter how great it is, cannot make history by itself; for it is the collective effort of the group under wise leadership that can achieve greatness. Only the Prophets were fully supported by direct Divine care which drew for them the path of attraction, filled their hearts with resoluteness and made them better able to endure hardships and pass difficult trials. Nonetheless, when the power of the remarkable spiritual leaders, the determined ones, is well settled it becomes like the sun, its light covers the horizon and reaches the crowds, energizing the hearts and preparing them for action and construction.

There is no doubt then that the spirit of faith is ablaze within the hearts of the possessors of resolution, the makers of history; for they are the productive stations which feed the whole location with its light. The most important characteristic that distinguishes these historical figures is their witty way in leading people and their consistency in acting piously.

Wit is an unlimited power that illustrates plans, supervises the way, and provides methods that can grant prosperity and success in what they strive for. When the consistent intellect continues within an individual or a group, it becomes possible to find a solution for any emergency, difficulty or pressing obstacle. Genius is no more than the ease by which great visions come true and by which the most impressive results are engraved upon the community. Wherever the pen rolls in the hand of the genius, catalogues of detailed illustrations and meaningful images appear to his insightful eye. A genius has a piercing intuition and he collects within his soul faculties that can carry many Divine gifts within it. By a direct connection that drives him, he can embrace the apparent and the hidden spiritual and social needs in his surroundings with a deep level of comprehension and with the breadth of its boundaries.[43] Genius is a fantasy that stuns us wherever and whenever it appears and in whatever form it manifests. Just as the individual can be prepared for the lofty ethics through discipline and purifi-

---

[43] Gülen, *Wa Nahnu Nuqimu Sarh ar-Ruh* (As We Are Erecting the Edifice of Our Spirit), p. 79.

cation, nations can play their magnificent roles and attain glory through discipline and training mankind to overcome danger and obstacles by facing up to what makes the ego proud.

Gülen's Discourse on the Community of the Qur'an

The honor that Allah bestowed on the Muslim nation is that He made it the community of the Qur'an. The preserved Holy Book was for this nation the greatest incubator, the most knowing care-giver and the purest guide. In any era the call for awakening has always counted on success by following the guidance in the Qur'an. Success was granted when the call followed its teachings closely and as long as it continued to seek wisdom from the Qur'an.

In general, most generations of Muslims testify to the glory of the Qur'an and its miraculous effect which relies on its apparent motivational pedagogy that speaks to the Muslim reader urging him to contemplate, to reflect, to reason and construct his ability to deduce, which analyzes the phenomena and examines the laws.

A few of the key phrases in the Qur'an which are often repeated either to urge, stimulate, scold or order are "Cannot they reason?" and "Cannot they reflect?" and "Cannot they contemplate?" and "Do they not travel through the earth, and see what was the end of those before them?"

There are many places in the Qur'an that speak to the intellect and raise reason to a lofty status, asking us to reflect. This is why the Islamic nation was a strong intellectual nation. If it was not afflicted by letting go of the Qur'anic guidance and indulging in ignorance which caused it to deviate from the essence of the Qur'an and lose its true understanding, it would have remained an intellectual nation, a nation of sound reason through sincerity and actions.

Addressing this point, Mr. Gülen says, "Contemplation is the blood of Islamic life."[44] He also wrote, "When contemplation stops the heart darkens, the soul is disturbed and the Islamic life is changed into a

---

[44] Gülen, *At-Tilal az-Zumrudiyya* (Emerald Hills of the Heart: Key Concepts in the Practice of Sufism), 43/1

dead corpse."[45] Intellectualism is a form of worship in Islamic law. This is because Islam made contemplating the universe, understanding nature and deducing concepts from what is clear a way of affirming one's faith and the method of drawing the blessing of certitude. "Faith-based contemplation of the universe is the place of blessings."[46]

Islam informed us of the main principles of its creed. Allah sent down the chapter al-Ikhlas, and affirmed its signs (*ayat*) as in His saying, "*Say: He, Allah, The One*" (al-Ikhlas 112:1), and in His saying, "*Allah, there is no deity but He, the Living, The Self-Subsisting*" (al-Baqarah 2:255). Then, He demanded the faithful believer to deduce the signs of monotheism; for unity is the underlying manifestation in nature and in the universe around him. This means that, "The peak of reason is the realization of the existence of Allah which also begins with Him, Transcendent and Mighty is He."[47] In both cases, the individual contemplating reality is appointed to succeed in his pursuit like the soil that prospers, producing its fruit whether the rain comes early or comes late!

There is no doubt that the possessors of faith-based insight easily touch the illuminating spirit where the spirit of the Qur'an is embodied. They grasp the logical method by which its truth is presented. Mr. Gülen says, "Indeed, those who work in the field of knowledge, knowing, and wisdom read this Glorious Book with desire and ecstasy; for they witness its clarification of the secrets of existence and the most subtle matters that exist within the essence of nature which the Qur'an puts right in front of their eyes."[48]

The Qur'an highlights the apparent in its easy and clarifying way. It elaborates on purposes by pointing out the interconnection between the visible and the hidden realms and it is not satisfied by stopping with only what is manifest, but it opens the mind to realities by which all illusions and falsehoods are destroyed and it establishes in its place a clear awareness and knowledge of that which is absent from our imme-

---

[45] Ibid.

[46] Ibid., 45/1

[47] Ibid., 46/1.

[48] Gülen, *Taranimu Ruh wa Ashjanu Qalb* (The Soul's Hymns and the Heart's Sentiment), p. 59.

diate perception—the unseen which takes the correct position in one's conscience. Thus, the Qur'an is the teacher of the mind and the guide for the soul. It demands from us methods of true reasoning. "Indeed, the Qur'an addresses all aspects of existence in depth, clarifying them and explaining their purposes, their constitutions and foundations in a way that leaves no ambiguity or doubt."[49] This is because, "The Qur'an addresses the life of the core being, the spiritual and the intellectual life of the human being. It regulates it by showing the human being the loftiest goals, taking him by the hand to attain these goals."[50]

This method of gradual unveiling is what distinguishes the authenticity of the Qur'an because it is particular to it. The inclusiveness of its knowledge is not limited to the senses or the experimental which are equal faculties in all human beings. It takes the intellect to the first principles putting it face to face with knowledge of the sacred metaphysical realm where it is guided to know the Doer of it all or the Creator, the Lord of the heavens and the earth. This gnosis can liberate the human being from the bondage of the illusions that chained him and made him a soul in worship with the created phenomena. When the Qur'an turns the attention to the reality of the cosmological system that contains galaxies, and planets such as the sun, the moon and the stars, it confirms their subjugated functions. In this respect, the Qur'an unveils two lofty realities at the same time:

1. It confirms the presence of the existent entities
2. It identifies its physics as part of the universe which has a particular function in life and in nature

The Qur'an affirms the favor of the One who brought it into existence as a gift for us. At the same time, it points out the responsibility that Allah asks from us towards it. Allah commands us to take it as a medium that affirms our faith in Him and He also commands us to be His representatives in the universe who perform pious, responsible and constructive actions. The Qur'an gives this guidance to people. It opens a gap which causes the edifices of ignorance, confusion and polytheism

---

49 Ibid.
50 Ibid.

to collapse. It enables the mind of man to remove the veils of illusion and falsehood and open his eyes to see the objective truth. In this way, people can know Allah, the Only Deity and be faithful in their religion. They can construct their relationship with the universe with all of its elements and denounce forever the culture of polytheism and associating partners with the Truly Real.[51]

Indeed, one of the most prominent gains which humanity has achieved by the favor of the descending of the Qur'an is modifying the perspective that man had for himself. The Qur'an restored the position of the human being as the center of the universe. It affirmed his vice-gerency on earth. With this modification in the propositions in the mind of man, his ideology is transformed into the stage of action and his freedom is based on knowledge and responsibility. He would no longer submit to the lords of illusions—nature and phenomena—nor to hidden or unknown causes which continue to confuse his thinking and worry his soul. Man realizes that he is the master of his own fate in accordance to his binding relationship with the Truly Real, the Sole Creator who is the Lord of the worlds.

In this way, all aspects can be unified in man's perspective of the world and he will realize the common fate of humanity. This realization brings him contentment and the warning concerning the covering up of the truth (*kufr*) becomes clear and understandable. The creed of covering up the truth or rejecting it can lead to an ideology of deifying the human being where individuals and groups control others. The creed of "the death of God" claims divinity for the human being which is an extension of ancient beliefs in which some human beings were worshipped as gods.[52]

---

[51] The fate of the polytheistic religions which are still alive today is to be annihilated; for contemporary man, even though he has the illusion that his advancement in science and technology will make him get rid of religions, will surely come to realize that he cannot live without a faith-based unification. Nonetheless, no matter how man arrogantly deviates from the truth of monotheism there is no doubt that he always comes back to it and we shall see how the future will confirm the certitude of man concerning the existence of the Lord of the worlds.

[52] We can see this in the creed of the ancient Egyptians.

It is known that an ideology tends to dynamically publicize its knowledge as well as the inspirations and conclusions that were made available for it in order to confirm its level of consciousness and to gain an affirmation of its beliefs. The teachings of the Qur'an stimulated and liberated thought from its chains and this was also the dynamic process of Islamic ideology.[53] Thus, it swam free on the horizons, illuminated by rules and steady in cultivating conclusions.

This is because the Glorious Qur'an serves the soul and the mind of man, purifying them from the illusion of polytheism and preparing them for sound judgment. The first Muslims did not have the chance to conquer empires and establish the Word of Allah in all places. Nonetheless, the Qur'an rejuvenated them spiritually and re-characterized them emotionally and intellectually. In this way, they were prepared to be not only the conquerors but also, "the spiritual guides for humanity leading it towards a Qur'anic civilization."[54] Through its disciplining and lofty ethics, the Qur'an created brotherhood between different nations and fused them together. "It is a Book that kindles within the souls the love of freedom, the understanding of justice, the spirit of brotherhood and the desire to help others and live in service for them."[55]

Time continues to reveal the glory of the Qur'anic principles and harmonize them with the soul of man no matter how advanced he becomes in science and civility. There is no wonder that today, as Mr. Gülen says, we can see people embracing the Qur'an at a fast pace more than we expected or imagined. People from many nations have been opening up to Islam and this is not a hidden fact concealed from anyone who can see,[56] and even though this is still in its early stages, the appeal of Islam has already started to make its enemies worry.

---

[53] This contribution of ideologies by publishing them can act to illuminate the collective thought of humanity as a whole. This characterized Islamic ideology in its early stages of civil prosperity for it crossed its geographic boundaries and reached many societies and nations and settled therein. A good example to look at the influence of Islamic ideology is Europe.

[54] Gülen, *Taranimu Ruh wa Ashjanu Qalb* (The Soul's Hymns and the Heart's Sentiment), p. 62.

[55] Ibid., p. 60.

[56] Ibid., p. 50

What attracts people to Islam in this era and will in the future is the fact that, "It is an easy Book of guidance for those who open their eyes to its truth. It takes them by the hand to dive into the metaphysical shore beyond this physical world. It breathes into the pure consciences whiffs of pure goodness at all times."[57] The Qur'an is a heavenly record that states human rights within the firmly established truth that has no room for prejudice.[58] It provides ethical standards that purify people's behavior and works as a bridle for selfishness and a breaker of arrogance.[59] The Qur'an teaches man how to be humble and how to live in harmony with nature and all of its creatures. It is the Book that has the collective thoughts of all the holy books; for it affirms the prophecy of all the Messengers of God.[60]

In addition to disciplining our bodies, the Qur'an disciplines our souls, minds and consciences. It prepares us to be human beings of the future after it showed us our origin from an atom, beyond visible matter and subtle bodies.[61] Our preparation for the future will not be complete until we fully embrace and apply it and until we contemplate it deeply and benefit from it as its first seekers did.[62] This is because, "It is a book that invites us: to know, to scientific pursuit, to contemplation, and to systematic thinking so that we can read the book of the universe and understand the secret of existence."[63]

Truly, "The Qur'an is the eye of the human being that enables him to watch eternity."[64] "The wisdom of sending down the Qur'an is to initiate a new pattern for today's man. The Qur'an pierces through the depth of the hearts which no other books have reached. It establishes faith-based rule within the hearts and it assigns the pathways to eternity to the destructive man. From the window of his heart and soul, the

---

[57] Ibid., p. 60
[58] Ibid.
[59] Ibid., p. 61
[60] Ibid.
[61] Ibid.
[62] Ibid.
[63] Ibid.
[64] Ibid., p. 183

Qur'an allows the human being to witness eternity and to taste everlasting happiness even though he has not yet reached the other realm."[65]

In this way, Mr. Gülen's view of the Qur'an can be defined; for he considers it the most important pillar of having a constructive and dynamic faith-based ideology. To him, the Qur'an is the most important reference that refines reason and plants within it a spirit of sagacity and discernment. The Qur'an provides man with a kind of faith that does not cause the marginalizing of life's affairs nor cause a loss in the value of the essential meanings of life. This is why Mr. Gülen continues to warn of misusing the Qur'an by misunderstanding it or misapplying it. What dragged us to the abyss we are in is our misunderstanding of the text of the Revelation and our superficial naïve ways of dealing with it. This is the cause of the decline in the minds of Muslims who started to receive the Revelation as if it were a story and not as universal concepts which have eternal purposes.

Mr. Gülen interacts with the spirit of the Qur'an with an ever modern illuminated mind. Thus, he can see how the Qur'an is the holy primary developer which cares for all the aspects of man including his finite and infinite aspects. He studied the text of the Qur'an as the holy epiphanies that stimulate a true intellectual grasp which expands the intellect by opening the door to its meanings and by looking at the style of its presentations as windows for the intellect. The Qur'an strengthens the faculties of contemplation and deduction. Mr. Gülen believes that Allah, through His masterful Revelation, brought a written and ever fruitful record that can feed the soul with its allusions, which the heart welcomes as inspirations rising as illuminating suns within one's feelings. By its allusions, the intellectual capacity of the human being continues to grow and his receptivity to be intellectually enlightened is activated. In this way, his conscience is directed towards the authenticity of the truth which qualifies him to live a life full of constructive actions, lofty ethics and pure goodness.

---

[65] Gülen, *Adwa'u Qur'aniyyah fi Sama' al-Wijdan* (Qur'anic Lights in the Heavens of Conscience), p. 161

Chapter Two

The Journey of the *Ummah* from Regressive Jurisprudence to the Jurisprudence of Renaissance

At the time of regression, the story of the world has become an enclosed religious ruling in its details and entirety. Each new thought emerging from it is mere imitation. The reformist confrontation to this regression is an essential obligation considering the literary accountability which it embodies as an heir to the Prophet.

When Nursi realized the reality of regression on the level of the country's leadership he hastened to object to it because it was an obligation and an immediate need concerning their positions and rulings. He divorced the system applying Allah's saying, *"You will not find a people who believe in Allah and the Last Day having affection for those who oppose Allah and His Messenger, even if they were their fathers or their sons or their brothers or their kindred"* (al-Mujadila 58:22). He then brought his activities to a halt and closed his circle of interactions and secluded himself. He avoided anything that could be considered support for the status quo of his time. He secluded himself even before the home arrest that was imposed upon him later. During his seclusion, he continued to illustrate the plan for refuge. Allah inspired him to write his contemplations on the concealed secrets of the Qur'an which resulted in his writing the *Risale-i Nur* (Epistles of Light) collection. One of its aspects is suggesting remedies for the diseases of the soul and how to protect the heart from spiritual illnesses and how to protect the self from psychological ruin due to losing one's faith-based immunity.

The center focus of Nursi's religious ruling and diligent efforts to legislate religious-based rulings was to be grounded in the concept of "La ilaha illa Allah" (There is no deity but Allah). This is because the aim of alienating religion was to amputate the concept of monotheism and to empty the souls of faith in order to fill them with a sterile wind!

The experience of writing the *Epistles* followed the guidance of the Islamic Call in its simple way. It had limited numbers of readers and followers at that time but as time passed many remarkable students and followers spread the *Epistles* across the horizon. This formed an opposing current towards the alienation of life which the politicians at the time worked to support at all levels and in all fields.

Nursi closed the door of *ijtihad* in fear of the invasion of non-authentic *fatwas* that the regime and its followers might impose to confuse the faithful believers and make the alienation of religion appeal to them. The waves were high coming one after the other from the front and the back!

Nonetheless, in spite of closing the door of *ijtihad*, Nursi continued to be fully aware of the new stages people were going through and he would issue *fatwas* in accordance to the emergency situation as he saw fit. Each new turn demanded of him a thorough reading and understanding of the Qur'an and a clear interpretation to his followers. All of his *fatwas* formed a behavioral journal of jurisprudence which he named *The Greatest Jurisprudence*. It confronted and destroyed all the plots to alienate religion from people's lives.

One of the greatest characteristics of Nursi's policy, which he followed and asked his companions to follow, was in its essence a jurisprudence of opposition and confrontation. This is because what was happening to the country at that time was not a limited type of harm to a few individuals or a particular group of people, but it was a calamity, a spiritual coup of religion which sought to transform the whole society and turn it away from its religion, its origin and its civilization.

Under these serious circumstances Islam was facing in Turkey, Fethullah Gülen was raised in a conservative family devoted to the Qur'an. With its desperate spiritual hold the family succeeded in carrying out its responsibility towards its members and their surroundings. The family maintained its religion and raised its children in a traditional atmosphere in accordance to the teaching of jurisprudence, the spiritual guidance of Sufism and the solid polite manners of the villagers. This helped the family to be steadfast in following its plan and holding onto the hot stone in an atmosphere that was full of danger where spying on religious people and limiting their religious activities were the norm. Anyone who emitted the fragrance of the Qur'an or of faith was restricted and watched.

Gülen: The Founder of the Jurisprudence of Renaissance and Construction

Today, Gülen occupies the front seat in the lines of elite Turkish scholars and intellectuals whose goal is rectifying and reviving the spiritual life in Turkey. This is their chief aim and what keeps their minds and hearts busy. In doing so, they follow their spiritual sense which still fills the hearts of many. The civil heritage, of which history shows each glorious achievement, continues to inspire. It stands as a reminder of those who carry the pride of past glory. It opens before them the horizons of a future that has clear milestones. It is a paved road that can continue without turning or ending. It is a path which has lasted for ten centuries and which was faithful to the spirit which granted the *ummah* its honored place in history and its leadership of a great civilization in the world.

Gülen represents a golden chain of blessed predecessors who emerged in different eras and places. They devoted themselves to service, to worship and to calling people to Allah. They exhibited benevolence and excellence in serving their *ummah*. This declaration of his loyalty to his prominent Turkish predecessors, who served the *ummah*, is the first testimony of the originality of the corrective way he is taking. It shows that he is keen on extending the living reality that the pious ones before him had kept alive as they served the Divine message. They were guided by their faith and accountability and by their care for the religion revealed to Muhammad, peace and blessings be upon him.

Openly following the right way is in harmony with the impartiality that characterized Mr. Gülen's reform doctrine and he has done this his whole life. He is one of the masters who abides by the rules of seeking, who annihilated the ego. They are not busy with the "I-ness" and with the desires that occupy the self that seeks to show off and be acknowledged. On the contrary, he is fully immersed in the pursuit of service and what keeps him busy is making a plan and a program for the renaissance. He does not care for position or fame which affects many scholars today. This causes those pseudo scholars to slouch spiritually and it limits their efforts and effectiveness and divides them and so they fail in achieving lofty goals because of their selfish concern for leadership, fame and rank.

Gülen continues to alert people concerning the danger of letting the ego be involved in performing services and of letting go of their lofty refinement and impartiality. This shows he cares about not causing any divisions in the society. This is because he fully understands the negative consequences of division when the *ummah* becomes fragmented into parties and polarized groups and when spiritual and intellectual intolerance separate people. This eventually limits the advancement of the whole nation because it causes it to lose its focus and its collective determined achievement.

Gülen's reform relies on a comprehensive plan that is founded on deep faith and belief that every sincere wise effort should not deviate from the general path which Prophet Muhammad, peace and blessings be upon him, gave its first light and push. Gülen believes that every leap the community of believers takes and every goal it attains in any era or time is only an echo responding to the blessed Prophet's call. It grants success to the workers and their fortune is determined in accordance to their contributions. Thus, they should not deviate from the origin or isolate themselves from the way of the Prophet, (Sunnah) which was in the middle of all historical movements in the *ummah*'s path.

Jurisprudence and Ideological Censure

The current in ideological Turkey changed and policy, not religion, became the maker of values. Thus, jurisprudence fell from its lofty height under the attack of rigid ideology. Issuing religious rulings was taken away from the hands of the qualified and the specialists and was put under the control of the secular legislator and technical administrator. They resist the Islamic sources and maintainers—the Qur'an, the Sunnah and the biographies of the pious predecessors. They discriminate against the authentic jurist and they abrogated his role and replaced him with committees they call "the secular center" which passes laws that encourage vanity and spread western thoughts and philosophies in all levels and fields.

Schools, media, and the arts started to broadcast the irreligious ideology to the society and to the youth. The reformer had no way but to start from this deteriorated situation which felt almost irreversible. A twofold reform plan appeared. Jurisprudence became only for ordinary people not for the elite. Thus, elitism and ordinary lost their previous definitions and no longer referred to the darkness and illumination in people as it used to in many eras of the Arab and Islamic civilization but instead became a classification method applied upon the whole society. The elite now refer to a particular group of people who are close to the scholar and who become his students and trainees. This is because religious activity became a governmental job. Nonetheless, this went on parallel to the illuminating activities of the reformers each in accordance to his readiness to sacrifice.

The activities of spiritual reform often took place secretly but they would spread light horizontally in an obtuse angle which started from the reformer himself, then it would be transferred to his regular devoted students who transferred it to their relatives and friends. In this way it continues to spread, widening the base of the pyramid in slow and steady but determined steps. The reformer had to stimulate the energies wittingly and cautiously with wisdom as much as he could; for the eyes of the spies were fixed on him and governmental security forces were ready to arrest him for the slightest suspicion.

How the Disgrace of the Muslims Started in the Current Era

The Western invasion which overwhelmed the Islamic countries removed the physical and the spiritual barrier that was between the Western and the Eastern worlds after the fall of Andalusia. After ending the Islamic existence in Andalusia, Europe moved into its advanced and expansive stages and it aimed at the Islamic world. It succeeded in overtaking the small but strategic places and it crowned its plot by dismantling the structure of Islamic vicegerency (*khilafah*) and transformed the Islamic world into a map to be colored by the powerful Western countries such as Britain, France, Portugal, Italy, Spain, and a few others.

The *ummah* suffered a powerful shock when it saw the Western armies invade its shores and occupy its villages and cities. All of a sudden people realized the horror of their shortcomings and how they had been fast asleep and unaware of history for a long time.

The invasion easily destroyed the weak army of the *ummah* and dispersed all resistant groups which stood on the front line of society and were the source of guidance to the *ummah*. Therefore, we saw leaders such as al-Amir Abdul Allah suffer captivity after which he was exiled from his country. We also saw al-Afghani who knew he was being followed by Muhammad Abdu. Many leaders were under house arrest and even those who tried to work under the care of the local governor such as Tahtawi, at-Tunsi, al-Kawakibi, Nursi and others faced exile or house arrest and their activities were forcibly restricted and the local authority withdrew its support from them because the *ummah*'s fate was no longer in its own hands. It was in the hands of the foreign invaders who carefully watched for any sign of wakefulness and suffocated it while it was in its initial stages. Due to this the Islamic communities lived in difficult times and were isolated from all elements of self-awareness and stimulants of renaissance and its leaders. The invaders executed their plot by spreading poverty and ignorance and by destroying all of those who tried to produce thoughts of resistance.

Turkey from the Role of the Custodial to the Role of the Ruled

With the defeat of the Ottomans in the confrontation with the major powers in the world at that time, Turkey's power was exhausted and its sovereignty was violated. Its army and politicians could not but walk on the road that was paved by the outside forces which illuminated its landmarks and prepared its plans and set up the instruments to execute them. In this way, modern Turkey emerged as an obedient student who followed the ideology of surrender and abandoning religion. It blindly followed the spirit of Westernization and separated itself from the *ummah*.

Modern Turkey embraced the new ideology which was an easy way to deal with the Western invasion; for it thought that if it did that for a time it would eventually belong to the Western civilization. The savvy Western leaders thought that by westernizing Turkey their plan to sterilize the *ummah* would succeed. This is because for a long time, Turkey was the head of the powerful snake they feared and it continues to be the danger that threatens them and so they had to subdue Turkey and they worked hard to integrate and tame its elites. They tried to transform the whole nation's Eastern identity in order to control the whole Islamic world and to be the masters of the universe.

They employed many circles to hypnotize people and spread the Western doctrine in support of the Western authority which was in control. Those circles worked to put the Turkish people in suspense so that they would not reach the advanced state of the West in spite of their Westernization and at the same time would not wake up to realize their plight and reconnect with their *ummah*.

The cultural invasion made a fake modern Turkey upon which suffering is written and it moves aimlessly between rising and falling. Stained forever by the regression of some of its people who betrayed the covenant and let go of their glory, which they had earned through successive centuries after they embraced the Islamic flag.

The misery of the Turkish nation is that it suffered spiritual annihilation and emotional destruction at the hands of a controlling few of its people who deviated from their origin and led the whole country into a path that contradicts the essence of its identity.

Many Muslim countries have suffered invasions and occupations at the hands of many foreigners as the West decided to creep into the *ummah*'s geography erasing its history and holding its future as it bet on keeping the *ummah* in its deteriorated state, bleeding spiritually. At the same time, the invaders continued to deplete the *ummah*'s resources which may lead to its utter annihilation. They saw the *ummah* as their main threat and an obstacle to their authority over the earth and a resistance that prevents the world from surrendering to their will allowing them to use its resources for the prosperity of their own civilization.

The Ottomans stopped their long confrontation with the West because of incompetency. Thus, its geopolitical front was destroyed and so Turkey lost its strategic and spiritual position and its role greatly shrank on land and on sea. It had no choice but to surrender to the plan of Westernization. In this way, Turkey entered a phase of self-destruction. In a few decades, the cultural invaders tried to transform the Turkish people to secular people by cutting every connection between them and their past, their *ummah* and their beliefs. In this time of disaster, Turkey had to react to the confusing and contaminating policies that were imposed upon it. Thus, a line of scholars appeared who confronted the plot and tried to oppose it even if it meant death. Their own lives became a cheap price for defending and maintaining their origin and identity.

The scholars of that era tried to confront the Westernizing policy with a faith-based Turkish policy. It was their fate to sacrifice their own souls for holding tight to their beliefs. Many cities, villages and streets witnessed the corpses of religious scholars, jurists and Sufi gnostics hanging from the gallows in order to terrorize people and warn them from opposing the doctrine of alienation.

The role of the scholars and reformers at that stage was to oppose them and inspire individuals and groups to unite and hold tight to their religion and not to surrender to the policies and call of integration!

Indeed, among the reformers during this era of commotion was the prominent warrior, Nursi who was on the front line. He spent his whole life confronting these policies and in laying the first bricks to reconstruct the protective spiritual wall that is able to resist regression. His biography was related to us in detail exemplifying the furious battle which the people of Allah were involved in. All the events in his biography show the furious attack he faced and that the plot to Westernize Turkey was set in motion without any wavering or retreat in completing it.

In this atmosphere the jurisprudence of seeking Allah's protection emerged and a religious ruling that allowed people to hide their faith and beliefs was issued. The reformers followed diverse methods of resistance. They sought to protect people and to allow them to declare their beliefs in accordance to what the situation demanded. They guided people carefully. Nonetheless, the media amputated their tools and chased their gatherings. It suffocated the voice of truth through killing the faithful believers or imprisoning them.

In these dark times, Fethullah Gülen grew up and was educated in how to defend his faith and beliefs. He was raised feeding on the original values and on holding firmly to his faith and he learned how to be involved in spiritual battles. When he became a young man, he immersed himself in the field of summoning people to Allah and stood firmly in the front line, awakening people spiritually.

Following the Doctrine of the Greatest Jurisprudence

In the midst of this ideological invasion, standard jurisprudence came to a halt and secularism replaced it as the new standard. The aim was not to cause limited change but it was a piercing attack that was aimed at all ethics and values. The Westernizing culture sought to uproot an existing civilization which had its history and laws and replace them with a new lifestyle that was a detailed copy of the Western lifestyle.

In this situation, the reformer had to become like a traffic light who knew when to give a green light to the passersby to cross the road safely. Their reformist confrontation with the invaders was challenging for they were less in number and in tools. Nonetheless, they began by qualifying themselves first and being steadfast in following their beliefs, they prepared themselves to hold the hot stone under the restricting scrutiny they faced in the new Turkey. Many Turkish scholars fell under the pressure of temptation or terror after the coup, while others devoted themselves to deepening their knowledge of the Divine law and the original sciences. In addition to that they sought to strengthen themselves with modern scientific knowledge of the time.

Thus, the reformers had to study deeply the secular philosophies which were officially declared as enlightening at that time. This was a way of qualifying themselves to refute and rebut them in order to protect the religion and rescue the youth with a faith-based philosophy that is based on gnosis and affirmed knowledge. At the same time, the reformers armed themselves with attractive ideologies that are based on tolerance and dynamic interactions with all ages and social levels.

They were chased, scrutinized and arrested and many of them were killed. Nonetheless, in spite of all the challenges and suffering their bitter battle was successful. They won the battle and their determination to die for their beliefs appealed to increasing numbers of the Turkish people. This was due to their civilized dialogue with ordinary people. The reformers merged with people and interacted with them renewing the past scholastic approach of the spiritual leaders who mixed with their followers and devotees.

This is what the prominent caller and struggling jurist, Fethullah Gülen, the spiritual leader of reform, renaissance and servitude seen in Turkey today, did. His biography reflects the types of preparations he made. After he was hired for an official religious position, he started his illuminating mission following his insights and at the same time he continued to acquire knowledge of both modern and traditional sciences. He left elementary school before he finished his third year, however, his devotion led him to attain the highest level in acquiring both religious and scientific knowledge. He was also involved in writing and publishing research in how to establish a faith-based ideology. He wrote about the Prophet's biography, history, philosophy, education and how to invite people to Allah and about biology. He also wrote on the subject of reviving the civilization and addressed issues related to modern science[66] and most of its particular branches. In addition, he wrote on epistemology affirming his faith-based direction and protecting it. His writing reveals the depth of his contemplation and originality as well as his being well-read in literature, cultures and the world's philosophies.

His intellectual readings were the source of deducing values, ethics and rules. His book about the Messenger is an example of his originality, and his civil, legislative and strategic approach. In his book, he revived the values of the Divine law, ethics, economic justice, and freedom for all people. He emphasized a guided equity between man and women. He also explained the art of domestic and international policy and how to protect the environment. Moreover, he pointed to the path of spiritual ascent and how to discipline the self and the major and the minor struggle (jihad). He wrote about social sciences and the jurisprudence of balancing the hearts, the cultures and the secular systems. He talked about materialism and metaphysics. Thus, his study of the Prophet's biography did not veil him from life and the challenges in his era and he did not become an ascetic escaping life and its hardships. He lived the Prophet's biography as a golden record that served as a reference for the renaissance he was pursuing and a revival he was hoping for.

Gülen, the reformer, witnessed the hostile invasion which suffocated the community of believers at all levels and he tirelessly continued to offer emergency spiritual healing, emotional support and protective services. The role of the traditionalist jurist had changed and the reformer had no revered counsel for people who needed religious rulings to contact, to ask and listen to the Divine law answering through his tongue, but the reformer himself had to seek people in an atmosphere that was suffocating the breath of religious scholars and spiritual leaders. He had to attract individuals and groups to him so that he could offer them a faith-based immunity vaccine so they could be protected from the epidemics and diseases spreading in the society.

---

[66] See his book concerning Darwin's theory of evolution and natural selection, *Haki-katu'l-Khalq wa Nazariyyatu'l-Tatawur* (The Truth of Creation and the Theory of Evolution).

Gülen's speeches changed in accordance to the restrictions of censure and spying. Nonetheless, he continued to consistently attract people to faith in accordance to Divine guidance. Naturally, the number of people who would attend the secular programs started to decrease as people began to go to the mosques. This was the fruit of the reformer's restricted efforts which demanded him to continue to teach. His mission was hard and discouraging; for people could not attend his lessons because they were under tremendous pressure. This is because the student himself who sought the religious sciences was exposed to danger as well. Thus many families tried to prevent their sons from attending these hidden classes for religious education. However, patience and persistence granted success to the reformer's efforts which also ended by producing fruit.

Because of Gülen's cautious effort he succeeded in making an atmosphere that encouraged education. The circle was formed and the first seed for the devoted seekers was planted. With time, this circle multiplied across the country through the volunteer efforts of sincere students. The bond between him and the youth was strengthened with time and its rope extended across Turkey and it even crossed Turkey's borders and reached Turkish people who had migrated to different areas of the world. Constructive projects, that aimed towards forming more circles of excellence and benevolence on all the continents, eased the establishment of servitude and emissary missions for Islam

One of the consistent traits of the elected reformer is working tirelessly to achieve spiritual refinement in his life. In this way, he truly becomes the golden chain that connects between the generations of the predecessors and the current generations. He becomes a noble dignified spirit that drives its luminosity, radiance, energy and blessings from all sources of faith. His soul is enriched with mastery through following the example of the family of the truth and its figures starting with Muhammad, peace and blessings be upon him, and his noble Sunnah and then following the lines of those who strove for the truth after him in every era. In this way, he became an extraordinary man that radiates light upon the earth and its spacious horizons. This is because his ego was broken by his impressive effort and that qualified him with the the identity of the complete human being (*al-insan al-kamil*).

This transformative effort, which the reformer exerts, is a chance to construct an identity that is being supplied and is supplying. This means that he continues to strive to receive the fortune of diamonds which he pours from the Sacred Springs, the Qur'an and the Sunnah, following in his pursuit the role models of those who arrived at the Divine Presence. Thus, he returns to the world with the booty after battling his own ego and he puts the diamonds in front of the world.

The love of fame which we see in people of this world transforms into the love of annihilation in the ideal predecessors and being unified with them. They immerse themselves in embodying their modal behavior, following their steps and achievements through the purification of the soul, the heart and the mind with their every breath. This makes the follower equivalent to whomever he follows. It makes of the origin, a branch and makes of the chain an example and maintainer. The goal of performing every obligatory or voluntary rite is to attain the lofty level of the ideal ones (*ahl al-kamal*).

Indeed, the exerted effort to surround the self with lofty role models from among the ideal ones is the difficult pursuit of the pious servant who leads the *ummah*. The discipline and training the reformer gives us starts with him, through self-discipline and training to refine his soul to reach the top and be close to the inhabitants of the unseen realm who appear to him at that level. At this level, it is not difficult for him to lead people. Thus, the power he exerts in leading is the same power of the eternal pious and righteous souls.

The level of interpreting, embodiment and inspiration which the reform preacher offers is an aspect of spiritual and psychological stimulations of the self by which he joins the possessors of resoluteness. Thus, we see that Gülen's interpretation of the noble Sunnah reveals his own loftiness and refinement which the Messenger called for and made it lovable to people. Gülen's devotion for the school of Sunnah was driven by an overwhelming will to embody the Sunnah in its minor details in order to digest the ethics of the glorious one and to take him wholeheartedly as a role model for his life and his emissary.

Surely, the level of deduction and comprehension by which Mr. Gülen interpreted the events of the noble Sunnah and the deterring lessons he derived from them, is the foundation upon which he constructed his whole understanding of the religion. Upon this foundation, he established the pillars of moderation, modesty and ease which the Sunnah and therefore Mr. Gülen call for.

The Ease of the Legislative Rules and Their Creative Essence

The driving force for ease, which Mr. Gülen calls for, is not to lower the standard or loosen the Divine law or to correct it as occurred in some religions that became divorced from daily life. For example, look at the rules of marriage and divorce in Christianity. But the real meaning of easing is a desire to return to the fundamental rule of the religion of the truth. The Islamic motto concerning this is exemplified in the noble hadith which is also supported by examples from the Prophet's life. He said, "Ease and do not make difficulties." And he also said, "Give good news and do not repulse people (away from the religion)."[67] In addition, he said, "By Allah I am the one who reveres Allah most and is most conscious of Allah among you, but I fast and I break my fast. I pray and I lay down. I marry women. Thus, whoever turns away from my way (Sunnah) is not one of me."[68] Moreover, he said, "Indeed, the Qur'an was sent down in seven accents so read only that which is easy (on you)."[69]

Without doubt, the Messenger lived religion on two levels. One level was of those who were purified, selected and protected and so his worship was ideal and complete and none can attain that level. The other level was as an ordinary human being. So, his teachings reflect the practical and moderate and balanced way which he wanted the *ummah* to live by in holding onto the Divine law and in embodying its princi-

---

[67] Reported in *Sahih al-Bukhari*, p. 27 and in *Sahih Muslim*, p. 1220.
[68] Reported in *Sahih al-Bukhari*, p. 1581 and in *Sahih Muslim*, p. 930.
[69] Reported in *Sahih al-Bukhari*, p. 696 and in *Sahih Muslim*, p. 515.

ples in obligations and interactions. He said, "This religion is first so delve into it gently."[70]

Thus, inclining to more restrictive forms of worship is permissible but it depends on the individual's determination. Demanding it of others is dangerous because people may be burdened by that which they cannot endure. This is why we see that Mr. Gülen emphasizes the ease inherent in the Divine law. "Ease is the spirit of religion. So, whoever wants to make religion difficult to the extent that makes it intolerable, would himself be crushed under such a heavy burden, while religion is living in straightforwardness that is easy and simple."[71] He says, "Religion is very easy and whoever overburdens himself in his religion will not be able to continue in that way."[72]

There is no doubt that the Divine law by which Gülen lives and interacts accordingly is the ultimate standard. He lives in devotion as a pure example. The level he attained and the fruits which his heart earned would not allow him to call for extremism. On the contrary, we see him demonstrate a spiritual philosophy that makes the moderate, tolerant and pure religion the base of life and the manifestation of genuine faith.

Gülen is one of the front liners who believes in calling the whole world to Islam but this should not make us think that his call for tolerance and moderation is to gain new Muslims. His perspective is that the attitude and behavior of Muslims can be inviting to Islam in itself. Thus, the Muslim's civility, education and ethical manners are invitations to Islam. The Muslim's interaction and response to the environment he lives in and to the events that occur in society are means by which people are invited to embrace Islam. Being a good example is the way to turn people's attention to the reality of Islamic rules. Allah did not prepare these rules except as a mercy for all the worlds. This is because He completed its pillars. It does not need a group of people to call for it but it needs a group of people who embody it and show it to people

---

[70]   Reported by Imam Ahmad in his *Musnad*, p. 3147.
[71]   Gülen, *An-Nur al-Khalid* (The Eternal Light, Muhammad, The Pride of Humanity), p. 586.
[72]   Reported in *Sahih al-Bukhari*, p. 15 and by Imam Ahmad in his *Musnad*, p. 4919.

in their manners and ethics and this will allow it to spread and appeal to others. This is because the example of ideal behavior is the shortest way to people's hearts without any need to proselytize or talk about it.

The validity of Islam is under great scrutiny today and there are many challenges for Islam from the transitions brought by modern life that directly affect man's stable values, established beliefs, and consented propositions. The media, which is under the control of many international forces seeking to rob people and nations of their consciousness, became the guide and the teacher that directs people and authorities. It became the lord of the family and the link to the world. Many fictitious figures in movies, programs and even cartoon animations become intimate friends to us emotionally and are able to affect our feelings more than actual people which we share life and blood with. The visual and audio culture pierces through our conscious and subconscious levels shaking our system of values which we inherited generation after generation. The effect of these ancient values regressed and was replaced by speculative relativity which the media creates and daily pours into us through its visual and audio effects.

The role of Islam is to grant protection to society. Muslim families cannot abandon the use of the Internet and the rest of the electronic devices; for even if these devices were not found in homes they would be found in cafes, in offices or at relatives' and friends' houses. So, nothing stops their horrifying effects upon the youth and ordinary people except if they seek refuge in religion, which when activated produces a renewed will, modesty, and self-observation within the self.

Truly, nations that are advanced scientifically and materially can provide balanced media programs for its citizens responding to the diverse tastes among them and fulfill the different needs of people, covering most of life's aspects. On the other hand, the Muslim nation with all its many countries is still suffering and unable to construct active, dynamic and balanced media activities which cause these nations to be more exposed to cultural invasions with all of their corruptive aspects. Religion is the only qualified tool to resist this invasion. An illuminating spiritual culture can help the society to have a wise say in what it receives and it can purify the media from corruptive aspects and choose that which is better. This live defense mechanism can reveal the reality of the validity of Islam at all places and for all times.

However, the danger is in the organizations and authorities who control the media. The world is like a big village now and the Muslim countries are the consumers of what comes to them through other cultures. If those who call for refuge in the Divine law are extreme and rigid in their approach and do not show flexibility, Muslims will not be able to benefit from their call. On the other hand, if all people abandon this call and neglect the religious factor or loosen it then the harm will be widespread and the whole nation will fall.

Thus, the call for easing and facilitating Islam is the way to reconstruct the Islamic society in a way that integrates it with the world not in a way that isolates it from the world. We need to construct an entity that is attractive and appealing but also protecting and satisfying which will cause throngs of people to accept Islam.

The steadiness of Islam is self-subsisting and is inherent in the ease of applying it and in its scientific and structural method which cares for the individual and the community. It consists of obligations and lofty ethics that are easy to see. Thus, having these ethics and fulfilling the obligations is left to the individual and the community as a whole. They have the responsibility of actualizing Islam in actions. The Muslim, to some extent, is led to the religion by the attitude of the whole community. Encouraging congregational prayers on Fridays is an example of this responsibility; for if the Muslim does not live in a community that establishes Friday prayer regularly, he would not be in harmony with his community. Thus, the attitude of the individual affects the community and the attitude of the community affects the individual.

Indeed, the spirit of mutual corporation, support and compassion is the obligation of the Muslim towards his community. This obligation demands of him to merge in the circle of the community not only as a social being but as a philanthropic being. In return, this benefits him as well; for without this spirit he cannot earn the spiritual and material benefits that the individual can gain from forming a bond with his community and society.

The mosque (*masjid*) opens the door wide to help the individual merge into the community. This makes the obligatory congregational prayer a noble and blessed step to achieve this union.[73] When the Muslim unites with the congregation he finds out that the rest of the rites can also be means for good ties and communication with others. The rites can strengthen the tie between the individual and his community. For example, the obligation of giving alms (*Zakah*), or the performing of pilgrimage (*Hajj*) and celebrating religious occasions can strengthen the ties and bring people closer to each other through all stages of life and events. Thus, Islamic rites open the Muslim to the community and harmonize the relationship; for religion is the greatest tie that can bind people.

Islamic rites and doctrine are characterized by constancy and steadfastness. Nothing new should be added to the rites or to the spirit of the doctrine or it will deviate from the Divine law. This makes Islam a pure religion that cannot be contaminated by the falsehood of renovation and deviation from the origin. Nothing within it or outside it can change Islam. This visible collective consent between Muslims gives Islam an applicable dimension. Thus, Islam is self-empowering in its essence and its spirit is ease, repentance when one must, and performing one's obligations when one is able.[74]

Because Gülen is a man of vision who has a universal philosophy of inviting people to it, he made the main rule for his doctrine ease. He sees ease as the original essence of the Islamic law and that which distinguishes it, but unfortunately people deviated from this principle which caused the effort of calling people to Islam to come to a halt. Thus,

---

[73] Let us not forget that there are many throngs who are used to attending the mosque with mere worldly intentions. Anyone can see people around him faking the outer religious crust. Soon, we discover that these people seek to gain people's admiration, confidence and praise which creates for them room to achieve some worldly benefits. These are Muslims in appearance only and they harm Islam in a way that can be used by its enemies. This is because they are hypocrites.

[74] Performing the obligatory rites is a must even when you miss them once in a while due to forgetfulness or lethargy or other causes. The gift of returning to Allah in repentance (*tawbah*) is a way of redemption which makes Islam, in addition to its other essential aspects, a religion of ease, mercy and forgiveness.

the appointed time of unifying nations with the religion which Allah willed for all of humanity has been postponed.

Gülen had to work to return Islam to his country after the forces of regression tried to turn off the lamps of religion in this society with its diverse levels. They created a foreign type of elites and social classes that fully divorced the religion. Spreading Islamic values was what Gülen continued to achieve for decades. At first, he was not allowed to discuss religion publically and he was not permitted to arrange meetings for dialogues to discuss beliefs, which would enlighten people and ease their way back to the Islamic creed.

The Westernizing force was not capable or intellectually qualified to engage in these dialogues and discussions. They were mere parrots echoing anti-religious statements which they received from the West, whose philosophy of materialism was anti-religious and some Turks just followed blindly due to reasons that are historically known.

Gülen suffered immensely in his confrontation with the fascists who did not have any logic or intellect to convince or debate objectively. They only had ridiculous slogans which they claimed would bring heaven to earth for the Turkish citizen. The secular culture became the only source for the brain-washed elites who were ruling Turkey. The self-claimed elites received from the West the spirit of hostility towards Islam. Thus, their priority became to exile the religious scholars and silence them. They fought the original cultural values and spread the foreign culture in the Turkish society.

For Gülen, the only way was to continue to work cautiously and to slowly expand the circle of the enlightened, considering the obligation of affecting a change in the ideological and geopolitical fabric around him. The Qur'anic teaching assured him that the power of heresy is destined to ruin no matter how long it lives.

Gülen observed his country's policy and did not consider the politics, which the minority held, of the Turkish authority and its extreme. The target of this authority was any religious activity. Gülen observed the different ideologies in the country and the geopolitical ties that were dividing the world into camps and forcing their authority upon ordinary people. Its allies were extended to different countries and continents. All allies were tyrant regimes. They were supporting each other and enabling each other to overcome any internal opposition. The conflict between the different internal and external ideologies was not but increasing Gülen's faith that relief was on its way and it strengthened him in his pursuit to waken people's spirituality.

The authority of the minority in Turkey viewed faith as the source of danger for their regime. This is why the fascists faced it with excessive cruelty. Thus, Gülen was in the front of those who were chased by the regime; for the fascists saw him and his activities as a threat to their personal interests and so they tried to assassinate him.

However, faith continued to be the hidden force which Gülen and the reformers held onto each according to his field and capacity. In spite of the hardships they faced they felt assured that faith was going to be revived. Indeed, Allah would not forsake the faithful believers. Soon, communism collapsed and today capitalism is suffering from ineffectiveness and tribulation and its fate will follow the communist fate without a doubt.

After the collapse of communism, the hardship eased and Gülen made his call to the Turkish people and many groups were ready to serve. They immersed themselves in inviting people to Allah (*dawah*) in accordance to the constructive ideology, of which Gülen had set its standards and philosophy. His long struggle against his ego and his self-purification had brought forth its fruit and he became a prominent figure in diverse circles of the Turkish society. Through his patience, wisdom, dynamic activity, steadfastness on the path, flexibility in dealing with reality, and his witty ability to deal with all situations with influential insight, Gülen became an icon of reform which always opened the way, and moved forward in steady steps. He continued to attract followers and volunteers. He became the face of a new movement, and a firm spiritual activist who influenced the society and directed it as a great leader by guiding it towards self-purification. The time he spent in self-examination and spiritual retreat made of him a luminous moon in Turkey's heaven and a symbol on the country's map.

Soon, governmental institutions opened their doors for him and prepared for him a way to communicate with the elites of political party leaders and diverse political activists who influenced Turkey's policy for many decades and exchanged power in ruling it. He led a civilized dialogue with the forces that continued to fight against him and oppose his faith-based direction. He succeeded in initiating a national dialogue that modern Turkey had not seen before. As a result of this fruitful dialogue and mature communication, many cultural organizations and communities, which have intellectual dialogues among all diverse currents, were established.

In this way, Gülen participated in designing the political performance in his country even though he never joined any party or indulged in political pursuits in their familiar sophistry.

It was easy for him to attain this splendid level in Turkey amongst his devotees. This was due to his faith-based life which he led with determination, his spiritual way and his blessed pedagogical system as well as due to his integrity.

Gülen became an attractive force, and a reference to return to. He had spiritual characteristics that gave him an effective dynamic power in the society. He had amazing interaction with people; he was like a magnet which attracts diverse parties with minimal levels of faith moving them to act, to compete and to be creative. Such abilities show a personality that can attract people's souls and a lofty essence that is overflowing with spiritual secrets, meanings and inspirations.

The success and extraordinary gifts of the people of Allah summon people to Him due to their self-purification and transparency which we learn about in their biographies. Their gifts are translated in the radiant relationships between the spiritual guide and the people. We can read in Gülen's biography about many praiseworthy benevolent actions which show proximity to Allah and reception of direct Divine profound meanings. This causes the hearts to deeply love the guide and this gives them strength, which they draw from the guide. This can be transferred to determination and the will-power to achieve and this reflects on their actions and achievements. This is a manifestation of the meaning of Divine blessing (*barakah*) and the granting of success which people can see and recognize.

This spiritual reality appeared in Gülen's relationship with the Turkish society. This resulted in dynamic constructive preparations for a comprehensive renaissance which included the fields of education, media, investment, servitude and scientific research.

This facilitated the way to open up to the outside world and extend the call to Allah to all continents, including granting scholarships to foreign students from the Islamic world or from any other country. This guidance concerning the enhancement of the *dawah* programs and the art of conveying the message was designed by Mr. Gülen during the time of globalization and openness.

Without a doubt, Gülen saw the outrageous degeneration of the *ummah*, which was caused by its deviation from the right way and its renunciation of Allah's rights. Only through observing Allah's rights can we protect people's rights and guard their dignity.

The major stigma which characterizes the degeneration of a civilization is defeatism which many Muslims have today. Muslims became passive, feeling humiliated and subjected to national aggressiveness. They lost their identity and are imprisoned in their bubble submitting to this feeling of humiliation. Trapped in triviality they do not even feel the disaster they live in. This demands constructive reform which Gülen aims at by reviving the internal spiritual being of the individual Muslim and reconstructing it on the original basis which led the Prophet's followers to establish a past full of glorious achievements.

Without doubt, a nation that has lost its values does not deserve to live in dignity, especially after it has destroyed its storage of dignity and distorted it by drowning in a state of lethargy in which humiliation is so settled that it is not awakened even with loud knocks. On the contrary, its weakness continues to intensify, "No great success or maintaining of success can be achieved at the hands of people who are poor in their humanitarian values and weak in their personality."[75]

The foundation of the renaissance and constructing the earth can be done by activating the potential within the human being and by

---

[75] Gülen, *Wa Nahnu Nuqimu Sarh ar-Ruh* (As We Are Erecting the Edifice of Our Spirit), p. 40.

repairing the spiritual cracks within him to reform him on a humanitarian basis. This was the mission of the blessed Prophet and was embodied by the Companions and the early generations of the golden century that followed them.

In Gülen's plan, the instrument for the renaissance and its form depends on reforming the elites and the youth to carry the mission of conveying the message. Their role is spreading the culture of enlightenment and revival. This is why Gülen wanted to provide a program which was a comprehensive model of spiritual and sentimental refinement in order to qualify those who wanted to serve the reviving mission. He wanted the revivers to be archetypes of spiritual steadfastness, devotion and pure of heart. This is because the most glorious mission depends on those who carry it out not for their selfish gains but as a representative of the Truly Real (al-Haqq), the King of the whole dominion who gives them this authority. This causes people to crown those representatives as eternal kings and the pages of history celebrate their lives and honor their names.

The fruitful preparations which enable a community to cross the lines of chronic failure which it lives in cannot be achieved except by arming the community with knowledge and the process of purification, which lead to lofty ethics, and by gaining a sense of the Hereafter.

Gülen constructed his vision of the renaissance based on forming an initial elite group that meets the qualifications of reform such as chivalry, expertise and accountability. The elites are like the horses that pull the wagons and so they must be well equipped with knowledge and provided with contemporary scientific enlightenment at the hands of the guide. They must be trained in the spiritual practices of the heart which make them feel the sweetness of servitude and taste the joy of giving and sacrificing. There is nothing more powerful than the heart's motivation to give and to be persistent on the path of reform and servitude.

Gülen realized that political ideologies are accidental faith that can soon be setback at the first hardship, challenge or disappointment. Ideology is then like a wildfire that does not preserve or renew. This is why Gülen focused on planting the spiritual values with the enlightened youth and within the hearts of those who serve. His writing supports his pedagogical and disciplinary methodology which shapes his reform and guiding vision which he sees as a must for the continuation of charging people with the vital energy needed for the renaissance.

There is no wonder then that Gülen affirms that only the gnostic who has knowledge of the Divine law can be called knowledgeable (*alim*). This is because Gülen understands the importance of religion in preparing the youth and in managing the inner battle and determining its result. For this, learning the Divine law is more important than any other learning. Thus, the one qualified to guide people is the gnostic who has knowledge of the Divine law and the religion.

No doubt, this vision used to be the Muslims' view in the past; for to them true knowledge was having knowledge of the Divine law and chivalry. Today, we see a regression and a change in this view because the balance of the matrix of knowledge has been disturbed. This has led to more emphasis on gaining worldly sciences and taking religious knowledge lightly. This is the cause of the ruin of the Islamic civilization. On the other hand, too much focus on the legislative aspect and neglecting worldly knowledge caused science to weaken and the focus on trivial issues and rigid systems. Thus, the spiritual, sentimental and ethical aspects of the *ummah* became arid and the chasm between Islam and Muslim became wide and this caused a great loss.

Gülen urges people to return to a balance of religion and worldly interests. This is why he finds the role of the gnostic who has knowledge of the Divine law essential. The *ummah* is now on the verge of inauguration and release from the phase of deterioration after suffering from spiritual injury that severely harmed it. The treatment must be essentially spiritual because the spiritual creed is the factor for the revival and the cornerstone for the renaissance. When the spirit is healed it will become easy for the *ummah* to catch up with what it missed in all fields of worldly sciences and civil skills.

Gülen's strategy gradually ascended toward its goals, realizing that the *ummah* lived generation after generation under the burden of heresy and denial of the truth. In guiding it, we should not focus on secondary aspects but we should rather focus on the essential principles of its religion and philosophical creed. Thus, we must advance our most important priorities over those which are less important. In Gülen's view, the creed cannot be divided but he still thinks that he must guide people gradually, those who became heedless and unconscious through the atheistic ideology, by allowing them to first have a taste of spirituality that makes them realize the usefulness of religion instead of initiating debates over secondary issues. Gülen focuses on the essential spiritual principles until people realize them and they automatically become ready to receive the full aspects and even pursue them by themselves.

Thus, Muslims should not rush into making the disputed points the initial starting place of constructing tomorrow in their pursuit of renaissance. Gülen argues for spreading the general values of the creed and to gradually establishing the religious culture that will widen the range of people's acceptance by liberating them from their heedlessness and guiding them towards spiritual maturity through a doctrine that allows them to discover the glory of their religion by knowing its humanitarian principles and its lofty ethics. If they are not provided with that, they usually turn towards the minor details of religious rulings and the minor disputes concerning them which causes sectarian division among them and becomes an obstacle that prevents them from completing all the necessary aspects of faith.

The Humanitarian-based Concept of Mutual Exchange

Gülen believes in people's right to mutually exchange humanitarian achievements and considers it as a fruit that can feed all humanity, especially in the field of pragmatic and applicable sciences. This exchange expands humanity's knowledge in general and leads to human development. If this development is based upon ethical, unbiased and non-discriminatory concepts, it will reflect its lights upon all of humanity. The usefulness of any scientific, industrial or medical discovery depends on how wide it can be spread and how many people it can benefit. Therefore, if development follows the right direction, it can become the means by which the scientists reach their own spiritual maturity and completion through their contributions, inventions and creativity. Spiritual maturity can help them care about the quality of their work and generate new sciences as they export their expertise across the world revealing their own genius and qualities.

Gülen did not develop this vision out of nothing, but he based it on historical evidence. The Ottoman Empire led the Islamic civilization for a long time with a record full of great achievements and unprecedented discoveries. It continued to export civil values during the Medieval Era, attracting experts from around the world and accepting many talents from all directions.

Through this awareness, Gülen believes that the stage of civil import does not mean halting productivity but it should serve as a bridge upon which the *ummah* can cross towards a comprehensive industrious stage that crosses the sterile situation which our Muslim communities are suffering from. Though they have become large consumers they do not produce anything of their own.

Nonetheless, our recognition of Islamic achievements is a living reference that continues to feed the souls, charge their energy and motivate them to work, to construct and to release their efforts to make the future and establish the edifice of an Islamic civilization.

The backbone of the revitalizing renaissance is full of clear traces and white pages which can become the ground for knowledge and the foundation for the aimed for growth. Being productive and fruitful does not mean to take unreasonable risks which would not enable us to succeed. Being productive and fruitful must stem from a wakeful state of awareness of the deterioration we have been living in for too long.

Taking all of that into consideration, Gülen sees the renaissance as a civil return in repentance to the Divine law, realizing our mistakes, our negligence, our regression and our disruption of the trust we have been entrusted with. Receiving modernity with all of its achievements cannot be useful unless it is associated with an awareness that is able to filter out the imported blemishes; for it was produced by a mind-set that does not pay attention to the Divine law concerning what it produces. This is because its foundation and ultimate goal is materialism. For example, we can see how the industry of making clothes has developed yet we see its deviation from modesty and decency. This is because today's fashion only cares for profit. If you look at the food or the medical industry you will find the same trend. The Divine law is absent in the industry of making food and medical drugs. They do not pay attention to what is not permissible.

Modern civilization is based on secularism, materialism and liberalism. Thus, anyone who has to deal with it must filter it to prevent its harm and to maintain their values from its pollution. The program of the hoped for renaissance would not be original and would not embody its perfect modality unless it pays attention in all of its inventions and exchanges to conforming to the Divine law.

In his books, *Wa Nahnu Nuqimu Sarh ar-Ruh* (As We Are Erecting the Edifice of Our Spirit) and *Wa Nahnu Nabni Hadaratina* (As We Are Building Our Civilization) a strategic plan is given which will qualify us to make a leap towards the renaissance. The servants of the renaissance must be aware of the basic foundational obligations in regard to their responsibilities and actions and in their plans, tools, goals, tactics and follow ups. There is no renaissance in making another's measures and goals of their civilization our own ceiling.

In Gülen's perspective, distinction is a civil condition that distinguishes between the collective Islamic identity with its firmly established spiritual dimension and other civilizations and man-made ideologies that are based on materialism. Religion is a source of inspiration and guidance. It is not, as some people claim it to be, to attain political gain or to escape from the world. Freedom without any measure and limitless liberty might look appealing to some shortsighted people but this is an illusion; for man will not gain anything from this except fleeting irresponsible pleasure that will exhaust the spirit without any everlasting benefit. What humanity gains through materialism is like running after a mirage by trying to rule out the Divine law; for they only gain an illusory image by responding to sense perception instead of responding to reason. It only satisfies their consuming appetite and fleeting pleasure more than what truly serves humanity; for food can only feed the bodies but the mind can only be satisfied by the precious realities that are like diamonds which time cannot affect. Measures, including worldly measures, can protect man from the fluidity of relativism. Thus, what can be more protective than the measures that are coming from heaven?

Indeed, the manipulating powers and the lavish careless minorities that search only for selfish gains are the source of cultural fluidity running after mere meaningless appearances and looseness that harms all people and violates their sacredness by throwing away everything holy. The space of deception is narrow even though those in illusion fantasize that it is limitless; for they circulate around their base appetites and whims, being mesmerized by cheap sources in miserable confusion like an ox tied to a ring.

The distinction required means resuming the fundamental concepts that can be translated into a grounded reality of excellent creativity, originality and actions that can produce satisfaction and surplus. In this case, even when one nation adopts some knowledge from another, it does not merely mean copying but it means adding to it and integrating it. Adopting concepts from other nations while maintaining the originality and uniqueness of the *ummah* is on the threshold of gaining new skills and confidence which are the foundations of transformation to extraordinary creativity and distinctive uniqueness.

Let us not forget that the date of the environment, the location and the dynamic social reality seals the final product even if it was copied. This is because mutual need is the determined aspect in producing new products in any field including new intellectual and ethical ideas. This is in addition to material products. All products, material or intellectual, are governed by the practical pressures that demand it in the first place and which lead to its production.

As for the chances for an Islamic renaissance, according to Gülen, the *ummah* has a historically acclaimed and civil depth of an ancient heritage in all fields that can serve as the base foundation for a constructive reviving emergence.

The collective consciousness of the *ummah* is still charged by the historical echoes that are full of accomplishments and a record of excellence and the tools that can prepare the community of believers for the renaissance to resume its honor and dignity. For the *ummah* that has a great heritage, its regression is like taking a pause before resuming its way. Thus, no matter how long the pause takes, the *ummah* will rise without doubt to resume its striving; for its spirit is trained for motion and continuation.

Conscientious Jurisprudence of Fundamentality and Amendment

Research in the exegesis of the Qur'an and the Sunnah requires awareness of their civil and renovating dimensions and is the motivating force and the essential focus of Gülen's doctrine. Many times, scholars who are focused on the theoretical aspects add their own speculations and views based on their own illusions or by mere adaptation from others' styles, opinions and quotes. Sometimes, they repeat what was said in the past or from the historical cultures and traditions of their own countries.

Gülen constructs his plan for the future on a solid ground which he finds in the Qur'an and the Sunnah but also from the lessons he draws from contemplating the history of the *ummah* during its different stages with all of its victories and defeats.

Reading the lessons in all of these preserved holy resources can shed light on deducing an accurate jurisprudence concerning the fate of the *ummah* and its eternal message. This field is realized in harmony with the Divine law which the Qur'an demands we take as a reference and have some people devote themselves to studying it and be in charge of it as Allah said in the Qur'an, "*For there should separate from every division of them a group (remaining) to obtain understanding in the religion and warn (i.e. advise) their people when they return to them that they might be cautious*" (at-Tawbah 9:122).

The climax of conscientious jurisprudence which, this verse encourages and makes obligatory, is a practical application of the daily supplication repeated by their tongues and hearts in every prayer, "*Guide us to the straight path*" (al-Fatiha 1:6).

To find the resources and the openings that can help the *ummah* to exit its abyss is a continual effort to infer Divine rulings and a thorough examination by a jurist who faithfully aims at rescuing his nation and pointing it to the best ways for salvation. In this respect, it is the greatest struggle (*al-jihad al-akbar*) and the greatest jurisprudence (*al-fiqh al-akbar*) which the *ummah* must turn to; for it stems from the original religious sciences. When the *ummah* adopted from foreign cultures then confronted the crusades, many philosophers such al-Ghazali and the philosophers of illumination as well as other intellectuals confronted the intellectual invasion and later the *ummah* was satisfied by fighting the enemies (jihad) and secluding itself. This did not enable the *ummah* to rise and strengthen itself; for seclusion led to regression and the complex results of regression narrowed the *ummah*'s vision and led it to more isolation which stagnated energies and made people satisfied with the minimal.

The daily intellectual activity in which Gülen is involved, is the tip of the mountain which all noble people must climb in accordance to the demand of their spirit of responsibility and compassion towards their nation, their religion and humanity. Thus, Gülen busies himself with studying the intellectual thoughts of those who lived their whole lives embracing their nation with their hearts, helping them to stand whenever they fell.

An intellectual like Gülen finds his philosophy from the concepts of his past and from the depths of his experience, recollecting the history of his nation which was written in its blood and taking guidance from the civilization that was built by its sweat. Gülen looks at the past or is inclined to it not because of inability or weakness, but because he finds solace in it and his powerful desire to tie the stages of the future with the past so that it will not deviate and it will not miss its aim.

The call for returning to the fundamental roots of Islam pulls him to hold tight to his base and roots; for history taught him that the path of civilizations was blocked if its wheels did not turn around the spiritual pillar. History taught him that civilizations that have a spiritual and sacred dimension failed if they deviated from the ethical path and turned away from its obligations. The fate of the Islamic civilization in its current state testifies to this truth and affirms its authenticity. This realization is essential in guiding it towards the renaissance.

The theme of renaissance and revival became the central case for jurisprudence. Its state presents itself to Gülen, seeking his religious rulings concerning the current situation of the Muslim nations.

The spiritual leaders of the past established the doctrines of jurisprudence, of worship and ritualistic rites. This was the culture of worship and was the ultimate pursuit for them to build their civilization. Today, the prominent jurists, "*and how few are they?*" (Sad 38:24) should focus on the jurisprudence of renaissance and how to establish the foundations for legislation in the field of awakening and constructing.

The intellectual of the renaissance must draw a map for the *ummah* to follow. He must diagnose the illnesses and prescribe the remedies, the duration of treatment and peace. He must supervise all the stages and follow up on all the steps as if he were a contractor who is constructing a city with all of its facilities. All work must be done under his direction until it is complete.

One of the enormous results of the path of ideologies as it ran towards a mirage of chaos is how the people lost their trust in their rulers and policies; for only a very few of the spiritual leaders interacted with the people and merged with the majority until people gave them the reign of leadership and guidance with love and certitude and followed their direction without hesitation. These spiritual leaders devoted their lives to service and people witnessed their giving attitude as they continued to suffer and strive through all types of deprivations. Very few of them even enjoyed marriage and children and did not even enjoy having a stable home. These are the signs of being Divinely selected and purified and it is these traits of courage and uniqueness which made them the Lord's without a competitor. Who could hope to be touched with the dust under their horses as they traveled the paths of the spiritual stations? Such spiritual guides remained steadfast their whole lives. They lived for the Truly Real by the Truly Real and not for any personal interest or greed. They are the possessors of resoluteness and completion. They grant us a sacred fortune which they earned with their sweat, tears and struggles, even unto death.

They chose eternity and kept cultivating double the reward and qualifying for it. They stood in defense of the religion with all of their power and wit at a time when everyone else turned their back. They received one hit after another to their original culture, to their pertinence and to their honor. They sought Allah's aid and were confident that the Truly Real will be victorious. They had sympathy towards people as they watched them being led in submission to the status quo and obeying the orders of the tyrants. Their hearts bled for the situation of the youth as they compared them with the youth who lived at the time of the Prophet and the following generations of the conqueror's offspring. Their voices rose, calling the *ummah* to wake up so it can reach the level of efficacy and mastery.

The humiliation and lack of development that befell their nation saddened them; for they considered this situation a violation of the first conditions of man and opposed the position of vicegerency and the duty that Allah entrusted the followers of Muhammad, peace and blessings be upon him, to hold. Regression and lack of development led us to slouch in our worldly affairs and our constructive pursuits. There are many knots that subdue the spiritual revival and awakening. Thus, we must work in a comprehensive way to treat the illness of the self from the knots of regression and their spiritual and literary consequences.

Gülen is sure that the obligation that is absent from our lives, is the obligation of civil renaissance and its literal rise. It is the duty of the illuminators to revive this obligation and to transform themselves in preparation for it in order to be like engines that can pull the train. Gülen realized that to shake the *ummah* and awaken it from its slumber in order to return it to the straight path cannot be accomplished except through activating the engines of revivals and through constructing the identity which is a composition of religion, history, and loyalty to the tree of Islam, which stretches to reach all of humanity without exception.

Mr. Gülen's involvement in service opened new horizons for the renaissance which the *ummah* has not yet fully embraced. Some groups, like the Sunusis, called for self-isolation and encouraged its followers to establish farms in rural areas so that it can grant them a level of self-satisfaction but this experiment did not traverse the plane of financing and encouragement and focused only on one aspect of its perspective.

On the other hand, Gülen's service doctrine opens for the *ummah* many broad fields so that those who are ready can employ their money, efforts, knowledge and any of their talents, abilities, skills and powers for development and excellent creativity. His soul, heart, mind and conscience drank from the Prophetic doctrine and the way of the early predecessors. This was in addition to what he drank of the teachings of the Qur'an and the measures of the Divine law. This transformed his life and personality into a living legislative jurist. His civil direction contributed to the birth and the manifestation of the jurisprudence for construction and renaissance.

For the first time, the pedagogic system of asceticism, spiritual retreat and devotion became divorced from the concept of turning away from the world. On the contrary, his spiritual retreats, devotions and asceticism aimed at awakening within people their faith in that which is absent from our immediate conception and a sense of the Hereafter that is directed towards construction and establishing projects to serve humanity in response to Allah's saying, "*Did you think that We had created you without purpose and that you will not return to Us? Exalted is Allah, the Sovereign, the Reality, there is no Deity except Him, the Lord of the Noble Throne*" (al-Mu'minun 23:115–116). And His saying, "*Whoever does an atom weight of good will see it and whoever does an atom weight of evil will see it*" (az-Zalzalah 99:7–8).

Many decades of inadequate thoughts accumulated, encouraging the attitude of resignation within Muslims. Many decades passed and even those who served the cause of construction did not do more than the minimum necessary actions. Their occidental lessons, which taught them the approach of the end of the world, caused the history of the *ummah* to come to a halt from the fifth century. Many of the achievements that took place after that were due to the awakening of the spirit of motion which had been regressing with time.

Nonetheless, Gülen's doctrine is persistently working today and it is rearranging the hands of the clock to the current era. He is paving the way of construction for many groups but because it is a new road, we can consider that every achievement that takes place is due to a new jurisprudence for construction. This is because the philosophy of service which Gülen offers is a philosophy that joins religion with construction and it resumed the civil perspective from the depths of the Qur'anic spirit. The Qur'an always joined faith with action as in Allah's saying, "Those who faithfully believe and do righteous actions." Moreover, the Qur'an, as in the chapter al-Ma'un (Small Acts of Kindness), gives social service priority over worship so we find the Qur'an asks us to care for the orphans and those in need before it asks us to observe Allah's rites.

The Jurisprudence of Financing

The service that was established by Mr. Gülen is financed by charity. During the period of regression, the society suffered from miserliness, but now constructive projects have been financed by charity funds and there is even a surplus. In the past, most charity funds went to the government and were spent on the palace and the army that secures it. But Gülen established the idea of investing charity funds in constructive projects.

His extensive reading about Divine law enabled him to distribute charity funds in accordance to the obligations mentioned in the Divine law to meet the demands of the current era. Financial services are a refinement suited for the present time. They form a bridge into social solidarity raising it to the level of excellent benevolence (*ihsan*) where in the past it was only done in emergency situations to rescue a family member or someone in desperate need. But organizing the financial aspect of charitable projects shows growth in a practical way that assures the expansion and success of the charitable projects.

This is because non-profit organizations can continue to live and act in accordance to a plan that assures the quality of performance. Legalizing the charitable work is important under Islamic law, under the jurisprudence of service. This is because initiating projects that create work and grant the continuation of services and assures the quality of management by lowering the money spent in administrative work, and setting budgets to finance projects is good organization which assures the excellence of performance and protects the right of the donors and investors. This shows that Islamic jurisprudence is not only concerned with the ritualistic aspects of worship. On the contrary, it sets the measurements and references by which each one knows their role in the Islamic civilization.

The school of service which Gülen established indicates the growth happening in Islamic legislative ideology. Through applying the jurisprudence of service, Islamic legislative ideology can achieve a leap in expanding its ability to produce new rulings that are deeply rooted in the civil renaissance and can aid further development as much as it continues to grow.

The renewal of civil services and their transformative dynamics fulfill the quest for distinction. We should turn our attention to the "Surah al-Kafirun" (The Deniers of the Truth) which governs the relationship between Muslims and non-Muslims. The *Surah* (chapter) says no to assimilation not only concerning beliefs but also in all other aspects of life. It tells us that the *ummah* cannot step into civility, productivity and self-satisfaction until it abides by what the *Surah* calls for. From this stance we can move with determination on a steady path to be in charge of our own lives in accordance to our Holy Book's guidance. This assures us respect, inspiration, excellence and pure goodness which allow us to occupy our rightful position in the world.

Chapter Three

The Experience of Service

A Step on the Path of the Contemporary Renaissance

With the fall of the Berlin Wall, humanity entered a decisive and distinct historical and civilized stage. Only a few countries realized the determined transformation that began to take place from that time. Many of the Arab countries felt that the cover was removed from their head by the collapse of the Soviet Union. Other countries felt that they lost their position; for the victorious Western side would not need their role.

Such polarization was a warning to people that capitalism would rule the world. Alliance lost its meaning and the door was opened for the new master to export its goods and demands to the world and that became the only way to win the master's affection.

At that time, our countries were like the ant kingdom when invaded by a plow that cultivates the land. They were like the mistresses (*harim*) when they receive the news of the death of their master. They looked around in search for a new master or for an imposter who would fill the absent position.

At that time, Gülen announced to the congregation that a new dawn had just been born and those who were willing to work for a better future could get started. This is because the path of globalization which the collapse of the Soviet Union opened would not last for too long. That day many heroes put themselves and their wealth on the ground in front of Gülen's platform. Engineers came with their expertise, contractors came with their tools, mechanics came with their labor and owners of factories offered their contracts while physicians brought their stethoscopes and penicillin shots. Teachers, nurses, graduate and postgraduate students stood together in the middle of the mosque listening to Gülen who was encouraging everyone to work hard and to donate what they could. There was an elderly farmer who put his rough hand inside his pocket and took out his old wallet. Some gave a few liras, while others gave dollars and many hands were competing to throw their money on top of the pile. Some of them were ordinary people who had just returned from their exile to their home country and by coincidence they heard Gülen's call. Others where old students of his or followers who were well acquainted with his voice as they had listened to it through his tapes that found their way to them. His words put them on the path and they joined the crowd with pure intentions and deep repentance.

Gülen split the pile of money with his stick into two piles and then he split each pile into two piles. The money was distributed to four groups of people and each group was dispersed to one continent. With these simple steps the project of civilization had started.

As We Are Building Our Civilization[76]

When we read the title of this book (*Wa Nahnu Nabni Hadaratina*), the word "as" ("wa" in the Arabic language) attracts our attention and the reader can interpret it either as indicating a starting point or a point of continuation. We also consider the words "as we" to indicate togetherness or a state of being. In addition, it indicates an emotion. These are some of the possibilities of how the readers may interpret the title. Nonetheless, in our view, the "as" (or "wa") indicates immersion. The context of the title indicates action, immersion, and continuation. Construction has already started and it is continuous. All the builders are deeply immersed and fully occupied by the project as if they were actually wearing it and cannot be separated from it. The doer in the sentence is the manifest "We" (*Nahnu*) and the one hidden is in the verb "construct." This emphasizes the meaning of being deeply involved

---

[76]   One of the titles of Gülen's books which was translated into Arabic.

and acting. This title gets its meaning from Allah's saying, "*Who are active in giving Zakah (alms)*" (al-Mu'minun 23:4). The title, as the verse indicates, means immersion and action.

There is no doubt that Gülen wanted to proclaim something in a very clear way. His title is like a media release statement. It contains the value of exhibiting and the eloquence of speech as if he is saying: Here we are. We started building and we are immersed in our efforts to build the structures of civilization. Here we are marching forward, excelling in pace and creative legislation as we did before.

Certainly, any reader who has been following Gülen's writings would remember the title of another book *Wa Nahnu Nuqimu Sarh ar-Ruh* (As We Are Erecting the Edifice of Our Spirit). The two books indicate the starting of blessed constructive work guided by faith and transformation and setting up the spiritual and literacy foundation for the *ummah*'s renaissance in order to resume the honor that it was robbed of.

Globalization and Counter-Globalization

When the global entities and powers formed their mega international corporations to control the earth under the claim of globalization, many youth and kind servants started a parallel initiation to set their feet on the path. They planted the seeds of service in many places in many countries in spite of their young age, few resources and limited experience. Their strong faith made them endure hardships and overcome challenges with patience, assured that aid and mastery are from Allah.

They learned from the lessons of admonishment they listened to in the many circles where Mr. Gülen delivered speeches. History shows that great work starts with small efforts which begin with ideas of a vision. These ideas with determination transform into plans and actions which take their position in the history of humanity.

Gülen realized that capitalism, which was spreading, would lead societies to usury (*riba*), market manipulation and economic abuse. These are all illnesses that are being spread by the new conditions but they will not continue forever. This is because all economic systems that are based on an unethical tendency to rob and possess will eventually fail. Just as the communist system fell because of its deviation beyond the boundaries of innate nature, opposing the logical spirit of balance, there is no doubt that capitalism will also fail because it is based on a cruel tendency that negates the concepts of justice and cooperation which Allah firmly established as the foundation for social life. Thus, all heavenly messages called for justice and guide man towards it because it is the straight way for self-satisfaction.

Misfortune Wealth

It was not logical that the projects of a few youth who wanted to offer services for people had to compete with international corporations which control the markets with their limitless resources and ability to extend their power on earth and even across the sky! Nonetheless, Gülen, the mind who prepared the youth to serve and who pushed them into the battlefield, was certain that what he was doing was based on a luminous framework which informed him that the hour of renaissance was due.

Communism continued in its arrogant ways until it collapsed without any resistance. This was glad tidings of the fulfillment of Allah's Promise to let His faithful believers who were forcibly weakened inherit the earth. Gülen was certain that destruction is the fate of every tyrannical power on the face of the earth.

Many of his speeches, in which he warned that tyranny's fate would be destruction, prompted ridicule and sarcasm from those who deviated from Allah's Path. Those proponents chased Gülen, discriminated against him and tried to subdue him. Nonetheless, he continued to strive and persist in his pursuit. Their claim of lordship only increased his strength and faith in a near victory. Soon, both movements, capitalism and communism, started to fall and their power started to decrease especially after their leading regimes were involved in aggressiveness and enmity.

It was natural that Gülen saw the collapse of the Soviet Union as a sign and actualization of Allah's promise. Thus, he did not hesitate to gather his students and devotees and push them over the horizons to make a new globalization, a globalization that has none of the material tools by which it can compete with the greatest powers in the world. These powers divided the earth between them and manipulated the markets for their benefits. Gülen realized that with these few groups he could pave the path which he and many subdued generations of the faithful believers dreamed about. Indeed, he had full comprehension of the lesson driven from the story of the race between the tortoise and the rabbit!

How Does Gülen Interpret the Events?

His faith in Allah was Gülen's source that enabled him to interpret the events. He reads the reality of situations and comprehends the motion of civilizations and their developments. He reasoned from the stories in the Qur'an, the biographies of the Prophets, and the pages of history what made him understand that tyranny's fate is destruction. This is why all of his speeches, his recommendations and his statements were directed towards assuring people that relief is on its way. After the ideology of materialism partially fell, Gülen with the quality of discernment which he has, directed his groups towards the right action at the right time. As a result of his brilliant initiation, throngs of faithful believers traveled over the horizons, spreading faith and inviting people to the path of Allah and offering services to humanity.

There is no doubt that when Gülen made that decision, he brought to life the steps of the Messenger of Allah as he crept through the field of the enemies who were directing their weapons towards him when he migrated under the darkness of night. These simple steps opened the door for spreading Islam to the Roman Empire, to the Persian Empire, to Ethiopia, to China and to India.

Gülen's provision, which allowed him to look at the future and have good insight into the historical path of humanity, stems from the Laws of Allah which are illustrated in the Glorious Qur'an and the noble Sunnah. This is why he was certain of the bankruptcy of the contemporary materialistic civilization.

Gülen's Call: Obstacles and Realities

Gülen knew that tyranny was narrowing the way of faith-based activities and fighting its workers. He also knew that the movement that he had initiated was not easy. Yet, he prepared the road for it in the darkest of eras. It was a movement that Allah brought into existence and none can stop Allah's Will.

Gülen realized that his service plan is a movement that has been continuous in time, even though he might have succeeded in keeping it hidden for some time. Nonetheless, the reviving wave that emerged from the depth of history had awakened him and revived within him the spirit. This newly born wave came at the hands of the carrier of the noblest Messenger and his pious Companions. Allah willed for that wave to continue at this time and to be renewed at the hands of many successive generations. Whenever the causes of awakening rise, the revived spirit that emerges from the honored eras reaches them and causes them to rise and continue the noble pursuit to the extent that Allah wills in order to stabilize His religion and His people who are the servants of humanity.

Gülen succeeded where many had failed, such as many theologians who took pride in their ideologies but at the same time were blind and ignorant of the rules of dialogue by which they could refute the challenging views. They tied their understanding of history to illusory ideologies so that they did not turn to the dimension of fate which is the firmly established aspect of the essence of existence, the lives of people, the flow of events and the flow of the stages of history.

Gülen was confident that the movement he was calling for would augment growth, quickly expand, and create successive blessings through which it can become an enlightening and constructive power. It will find its way by calling people to the truth and to peace and by expanding its philanthropic branches across the world[77] and reaching all people.

Globalization freed communication among people, multiplied its resources and narrowed the distance between different countries. This

---

[77] *"You are the best nation produced (as an example) for mankind. You enjoin what is right and forbid what is wrong and believe in Allah"* (Al Imran 3:110).

contributed to opening people's eyes to what each ideology was hiding. Thus, each human being got to know his fellow human and knew his position and limitations. Suddenly, he felt a deep sentiment that was created by many eras of regression and indiscretion. This sentiment is revived within the depths of people, pulling that which is related to the spiritual to its origin and pulling the flesh to its flesh.

The first throngs of servants arrived in the Arab world and started the constructive movement. People met them in workshops and in work places. They got to know them at the mosques and in the houses. Many mutual companies emerged and trade took place. All of this contributed to the revival. Many schools and educational institutions were opened and people crowded through their doors. The Turkish youth who were trained for service experienced the joy of working and feeling the common traits and ethics with the brethren who share their religion with them. Thus, they spread in broad environments on all continents. This renewed the common life which both the Turks and the Arabs shared for many centuries under one flag and continued to close all the gaps to protect their honor and heritage.

The authorities in Turkey could not see the criminal minds and the intellectual mafia that flooded the Turkish market with intoxicating beverages, spreading spiritual corruption, but instead saw in them businessmen with modest ethics. They saw in their movement a cultural economic augmentation that enhances the ties of brotherhood and friendships.

The ways in which the Turkish regime opened up and the ease which was given to thousands of men and women to visit Turkey in order to trade did not succeed in spreading morals that do not conform to religious ethics or in spreading Western-style liberation as the authorities hoped for at that time. On the other hand, the movement of service succeeded in stimulating the energy for working, the meanings of facing challenges, good manners and self-reliance. All of these values open the door of construction for the individual and the group, and encourages self-criticism and the realization of the reality of the political, economic and commercial restrictions that the society and the country have been suffering from.

The Arab groups that visited Turkey witnessed the reality of the change, the renaissance and the self-esteem that blanketed Anatolia. Nonetheless, in spite of the joy that this state can cause, it also evokes sorrow because of the absence of this spirit in their countries. They had not realized to what extent the policies in their countries were accomplishing every day and they were managed by elected parties. Islam, through the leaders of reform was in the forefront of the collective movement. Muslim politicians were achieving success that put to shame those who claimed that Islam was the cause of regression and deterioration and was accusing Islam of being rigid and anti-civil.

The results of connecting Turkey with the Muslim world was transformed from the fear of dissimilation and the spread of anti-religion sentiment to a realization that this connection can lead to originality, to action and to the construction of civilization.

The current Turkish renaissance sees rapprochement with the Arabs and the Muslims as beneficial. The rapprochement with Muslim countries can reverse the path of alienation caused by historical confusion under the claim of civility.

In its pursuit to extend its branches into the Muslim countries, the service movement does not want to overtake people's consciences or to tempt certain classes of people in the same way that many ideologies do when they expand their campaigns in order to interfere, to control and to influence the countries. The service movement tries rather to root the Turkish people anew in the soil of countries that are tied with it spiritually and culturally. It is like smuggling the sentiments, the feelings and the emotions towards the original enclosure and re-planting the identity in the ground of religion, on the ground of the abode of peace.

The service movement uses direct communication which shortens the stages needed. Gülen emphasizes using time well in order to achieve success and excellence. Indeed, joining the flesh with the main body demands the hastening of establishing the foundations and the pillars on the ground, especially at this time of a fast paced race and overwhelming globalization. It demands establishing mutual tangible and beneficial projects. Benefits should be felt immediately; for in every wasted second many chances could be lost and many fields might not be explored.

Hira: A Symbol

Establishing the first Arabic media in Turkey at the time of globalization, by which we mean the *Hira* magazine, carries many allusions. It came to restore the spiritual and emotional connection with one of the most important elements of origin; for it is the language of the Qur'an. *Hira* magazine is a symbolic teacher with all that this allusion means. Gülen supported this periodical connection because it is part of the plan for activating the rapprochement and joining Turkey not only with the Arab countries but also with many non-profit social, financial and cultural organizations by providing the emotional and spiritual support for this union. The symbol plays the role of attraction and encouragement.

Publishing *Hira* in the Arabic language in Turkey was a crowning stage after enduring periods of struggle in which the faithful people in Turkey were involved. They devoted their whole lives to achieving victory in the battle for restoring their spiritual and cultural identity. The ones who tried to alienate Arabic in Turkey wanted to annihilate it but the awakening, led by Gülen, restored Arabic to its rightful position. Thus, publishing *Hira* was an expressive sign and a clear proclamation that a new dawn had risen.

Gülen called for unity and spiritual brotherhood. He realized that many countries in the world would be strengthened by allying together. Thus, how could the countries that share the same spirit and a common history not unite to be able to resist the danger of assimilation?

Globalization has become a dangerous economic and cultural hole that threatens the weak and the disunited. Many countries who carelessly indulge in globalization without finding their uniqueness are exposed to annihilation.

Deconstructing the *Ummah*'s Entity

In Gülen's perspective, deconstructing the *ummah*'s entity does not mean to assign the leadership position to Turkey but it means uniting the *ummah* to be a strong entity and be protected against what Turkey and the rest of the Islamic nations suffered at the hands of those who caused Turkey's annihilation, codependency and humiliation.

The alienation that attacked Turkey injured the depth of the national sentiment and dignity. The Ottomans became mere followers of the sick aspect of Europe which destroyed its glory after its dissociation with the Eastern campaign. This is how the native Turk feels when he examines the last eighty years of his country's history. This is what makes him long to return to his home.

Thus, Gülen was also convinced that Turkey must return to its home. His conviction was the result of analyzing the different alliances that took place in the world after the end of the cold war and from contemplating the demands of globalization. Ideology is not the best solution for nations; for all ideologies are subject to destruction and change and so they are not everlasting. It is the harvest of fire whose flame is intensified at times and then fades.

The wise policy is the one that builds its strategy on constant conditions and elements that do not change with time. The tie of faith is a firm tie that is renewed in every era. It is stronger than a physiological tie. It is the homogeneity of civilization and a spiritual brother which is inextricable because it has wisdom and Divine management that protects the common interests of all people. Thus, it is very natural for the Turkey of today to stretch out its hand to its brothers.

After the Turkish people restored their awareness, they were sure that Turkey could not have a bright future if it did not seek refuge in a large national body that extends into a geopolitical environment as huge as the Islamic world. Turkey became an economic power that should be considered. In order to assure its growth and lasting development, to promote its products, and to guarantee bountiful assets Turkey must merge with its original natural body which is the whole Islamic nation.

The careful examiner cannot miss what Turkey is calling for and what it needs today concerning the establishment of constructive foundations and strengthening the ties with other Islamic nations through merges and exchanges. This will provide protection and strengthen all countries involved and help them increase their development. We have not yet seen any signs of positive response for the call of unity, exchange and rapprochement. This is because unity does not serve some countries' interests.

Gülen's writing emphasizes his perspective on unity and bringing awareness of its importance to the Muslim communities, especially among the enlightened ones who can feel the comprehensive doctrine that Gülen has, which can protect the nations and help them rise.

Indeed, Turkey is in the lead of awakening considering the experience it gained with its interaction with the West due to its geographical location. Turkey learned many lessons because of the cruel blow which struck it because it stands on the boundary with the West waiting for its European membership to be acknowledged. Turkey understood the chance which globalization offers because of its historical civilization. Turkey sees itself as an initiator of unity and alliance.

The pedagogical method which Gülen offers the nations helps them find their capabilities and shows them what they can gain from unity, alliance and mutually beneficial exchanges. It points the nations to the road of strength and how to seek protection in the preventive shields that can be activated through the sense of belonging and brotherhood. The hits that the West has given Turkey for its desire to join naturally directed Turkey to seek alliance with the countries that shared its original civilization. The rise of Islam seen in Turkey today was initiated by the men of service, guided by the spiritual authority of Gülen who works with faith and sincerity to continue in that direction.

Gülen's View of Civilization

No contemporary intellectual is equal to Gülen's level who belongs to a country which has been known for its prosperity for centuries. He lives in the time of an emerging contemporary civilization. He does not view civilization as all other contemporary intellectuals who do not feel they belong to the past civilizations. He follows progress from its midst seeing the severe consequences of abandoning the past civilization. He evaluates the causes and elements that resulted in the fall of his civilization and observes the current culture passing in front of his eyes as if led by an unwise captain. He sees the deterioration in the status of the Muslim when he regressed intellectually and denounced his values and how that stripped him of his key leadership position, which he lost. This transformed the Muslim to a submissive entity who fell with the fall of his civilization. This fall was due to his deviation from the path which the Qur'an and the Divine law point to.

The contemporary culture deteriorated and failed man when it aimed at causing him to rise. A great section of contemporary thought caused man in the West to deviate, making the concept of power and utility the basic ethical measure upon which man should base his interactions with people and with the universe. This can cause man to be confused ideologically and encourages him to claim lordship as the Greek lords did in the past. This illusion is due to the wrong belief in man's limitless abilities. Without protecting his abilities from inclining to his selfish whims, man cannot rise to his holy position which requires integrity. In this way, the West lives a tragedy concerning its relationship with the universe and all of its self-claimed lords who inhabit it.

For a long period of time, those who adopted materialism in the West continued to live as the Greek predecessors who claimed lordship and thought they had power over everything. But in spite of all the material gains he continued to act as a savage who lashes out at others. At the same time, Muslims surrender to a spiritless culture which halted their efforts to spread the Islamic message to the world. They lowered their energy and surrendered to humiliation. Their status was lowered to an extent that only satisfies their enemies.

It is easy to detect two types of cultures today: the culture of man who claims to be a deity and a culture in which man is passive. Both cultures are destined to deterioration and collapse. On the other hand, we find that Gülen illustrates the way to construct a hopeful civilization where man, as the essential element, reverses his state to the right direction. Gülen positions man to establish a new civilization that is free of the passive culture of the past and the power of the current material culture.

Gülen requires man to be in the position where Islam puts him: to be the vicegerent of Divinity. He puts his hope on the man of the Qur'an who affirms his servitude to Allah. He is the one who faithfully believes that he was brought to the earth to be Allah's representative. Thus, he believes in the essentiality of faith and service.

The man of the Qur'an is nominated to revive the authentic civilization or to deconstruct it based on three initial principles: faith, aim and time. This legislation which Gülen postulated as the foundation of constructing the virtuous city allows humanity to cross the slippery slopes and the tremendous challenges the world is facing today. In spite of the material prosperity which technology and scientific discoveries have given us, man is disturbed. This is why Gülen sets faith as the first condition of attaining a renaissance. He understands that different communities are suffering from a shortage in number. The development in the health field today gave us birth control. Nonetheless, there is a general increase in populations everywhere. This demands a plan to provide the places that suffer from a shortage in population with workers that are full of faith.

In its reality, faith starts with an inclination followed by an attachment. There is no wonder then that many ideologies can transform themselves through propaganda to faith. The faith which Gülen calls for goes beyond the emotionally based doctrines. Psychological research confirms that the strong emotions, which exist under totalitarian regimes, do not change. Thus, the ideological expectations focus on the senses and this is why its efforts eventually become frustrated and it collapses when faced with its defects which leads to disappointment.

The true faith-based religion means to arm one's self against emotions that come with success and failure. Man is psychologically qualified to indulge his heart in worldly chances to a great extent. They are prepared to sacrifice to win their worldly chances. Nonetheless, their energy changes at every stage and the enthusiasm fades away so the lines retreat. This occurs when motivations and reward decrease. These are the reasons for the failure and collapse of most ideologies.

On the contrary, when the motivation is based on a noble religion, the will to persist in pursuing noble goals stays alive in spite of the obstacles that might reduce its force; for noble goals do not die within the souls.

There is no doubt that when we examine the ideologies that are based on vain slogans we can objectively criticize them and highlight their errors and their deviations from man's innate nature which is in conformity with modesty that moderate religion calls for. The ideals of religion and its principles will always continue to be constant and radiant with their holy effect upon the souls. Only wicked souls fall short of recognizing the religious ideals. Our love for the martyrs stems from our love for those who devote their lives for these noble ideals. This lofty connection with the noble ethics and constant ideals is the spirit of religion which is renewed throughout the generations. This is what can make you the engine that does not stop generating energy and guaranteeing its flow.

This is why the contemporary regime fears the revival of Islam; even though they know it is going to happen without a doubt. They fear it because they know its power which exists within its essence as a spiritual organism that has radiated light throughout generations. They fear the power that it possesses which can energize the spirit of change after it has deteriorated. This is because people can be motivated by it regardless of the passing eras. This is because of the innate nature within humanity that inclines man to the truth. With this innate nature man pursues the embodiment of goodness which is the intuitive inclination to inhabit the earth and build a civilization which is the natural way Allah created us with and asked us to be witnesses, *"You are the best produced (as an example) for mankind. You enjoin what is right and forbid what is wrong and believe in Allah"* (Al Imran 3:110).

This noble faith, which connects man with the transcendent ideals, is the alchemy of success for humanity. With true faith we can raise pious men who join together in unity and volunteer whatever they own for the service of the community. Such is the man that is graduated from the school of the Qur'an who is colored by its nobility and ideals. Such is the man who can build a civilization. Gülen put his expectations on the existence of that man upon whom he relies to open the way for a better future. It is bringing religion to its pure essence by planting its applicable aspect within the souls and within the community. It is the way of energizing the forces to work and build.

Beginning the Call and the Formation
of an Active Human Being

Gülen's biography tells us that during his youth he was motivated by the benevolence and aspirations of his heart and he started to attract many students to his enlightening circle. He would help them understand their lessons and open their hearts to faith through his wisdom. His experiences were full of difficulties and required patience and persistence. As years passed, groups started to form and a communication style was developed and the circles multiplied. When the early students grew and became qualified to teach, they became emissaries for the call. Thus, the call reached families, houses and work places and it flew as water flows on land and wherever it passed, it nourished.

The period between getting the first student in the circle to the completion of preparing lines of emissaries in service of the call and their dispersion across the land was long. But eventually they spread over the horizons, setting the foundation for a happy future with persistence and determination.

When Gülen speaks about the time of transformation, he points out the hardship he faced in finding ways to communicate with people. It all started by sitting with one student he convinced to accompany him to the mosque. With continuous effort to attract people, this led to forming one circle after the other and the good word spread over the horizon. After time, groups multiplied and the service was born. Thus, there must be an initiation and that initiation might start with an idea which can be grasped by an active person who can plant it and prepare it to grow and become fruitful. It can all start by an individual whose heart is inflamed by love which keeps his soul kindled, dividing for him the road of examination and transforming him from one stage to the next. His steps are like those of the Prophets who are led by Divine guidance to wherever they are sent.

That individual can be joined by another then by a third and then by a group. Allah's hand is always with this unity. The faithful believers exert their efforts to plant the seeds of values and ethics which can prepare the souls to rectify their affairs. It all begins with making small corrections but with time these efforts can be joined and connected moving in two directions: from the highest to the lowest and from the lowest to the highest.[78] When the foundations are well prepared many fruitful projects can be established. In this way, the enlightenment movement can become a movement of construction, strategic planning, industrial work, as well as offering many other services.

This creates growth, prosperity and goodness in the society which attracts more people.[79] Every improvement which occurs in the social domain reflects a positive outlook of Islam in the eyes of the people.

School, Man and Civilization

We are used to hearing the intellectuals' and politicians' opinions concerning the role schools play in building the *ummah*'s future. Presenting this concept in this shallow way manifests a spirit of evasion that seeks to escape responsibility. They often do not really provide a way to make schools tools for building a better future.

Two centuries have passed since the beginning of the renaissance of the Muslim nation through which it achieved some success in the field of education. Nonetheless, it still imports all of its needs. It is still in the lower systems of education even though education has become the norm in the society.

Many countries emerged from their deterioration and achieved their renaissance in a few decades. For example, Japan did that even though many Muslim countries preceded it in trying to build themselves up. But today, Japan has become one of the major powers. Similarly, Germany built itself up after total destruction after war. There are many other countries that have accomplished success in the same way. Some of these countries are Muslim countries such as Malaysia and Indonesia. They stood on their feet and defeated the deteriorating situation.

---

[78] You can read an elaboration of this idea in Gülen's book, *Wa Nahnu Nabni Hadaratina (As We Are Building Our Civilization)*.

[79] In conformity of Allah's saying: "*You are the best produced (as an example) for mankind. You enjoin what is right and forbid what is wrong and believe in Allah*" (Al Imran 3:110).

Today, people acknowledge their remarkable success. What is the secret cause for these countries' success and why are we still suffering failure? If we follow their way and care for our educational and school systems we would catch up with them; for without doubt their success relied on an active educational system and successful schools. Nonetheless, does building schools guarantee the renaissance?

According to Gülen, renaissance cannot be achieved unless there is an excess of intense efforts where people compete to give and contribute and there is integrated creativity and initiatives. True renaissance is a constructive civil formation that demands constant motivation and energized determination to give birth to success. Such enthusiasm has to accompany the renaissance through all of its stages without stopping. Enthusiasm has to constantly flow through the society causing an awakening attitude within everyone and eliminating all factors that cause people to be heedless and lethargic in order to prevent the light from being extinguished, so that the creeping darkness would not once more overwhelm life.

The renaissance is a brilliant transformation of the people's states. The intense feelings which accompany giving birth must overwhelm all fields of life. Otherwise, the energies would fade away and the release would be obstructed. This could cause a further deterioration worse than the status quo.

The educational system is one of the effective factors which can prepare people for this hopeful leap. We cannot hope that a deteriorating and backward educational system will prepare the society and motivate people to transform their situation and use their abilities to create a better future.

All educational systems that make historical leaps and respond to the call for renaissance are characterized by spiritual renewal and scientific enrichment guided by a practical doctrine that plants within the new generation a heated passion for refinement. The successful educational system has to fill them with the desire for heightened development. On the other hand, relying on systems, mechanisms and channels that do not motivate people to change is mere pointless chatter.

Renaissance between the Ineffective School and the Successful School

The crippled school is the one that has a flimsy educational program and tumbledown epistemic approach. Its role would not go beyond a boring routine and mechanical framework. Its graduates would carry the same lethargic attitude which creates a stagnate atmosphere which has the same sickness that the school has. This darkens the social and civic status quo around them.

On the other hand, the successful school is the evolutionary school which keeps refining its methods and its graduates are active human beings. The school that achieves prosperity is a school that we have to build first so that we can have active and successful students graduate from it. We see how Gülen emphasizes the quality of the educational system rather than just building many schools.

The current educational system alone would not prepare a graduate who is able to give even though it is the first unit in forming society. This crippled school is unable to give us the ideal human being in whom the elements and knowledge required for success exist. It is impossible to find even one good example of a graduate from such a school.[80] This graduate would need more supplemental sources to complete the level of knowledge he could not get under the roof of the crippled school in order to complete his preparation and qualify him to accomplish the renaissance.

Traditional contemporary schools play only a theoretical role that has not yet taken a practical turn. This is because the schools were established within a polluted atmosphere that does not conform to the original values. The role of the educational system is to supply the social culture with the immediate applicable provision which passes from generation to generation.

When the school is saturated with the values that families need and the society as a whole considers sacred and when it celebrates the special occasions and feasts it becomes an embodiment of the collec-

---

[80] Gülen, *Wa Nahnu Nabni Hadaratina* (As We Are Building Our Civilization), p. 27.

tive dignity of the culture. The national and spiritual consciences circulate around it. This creates harmony between the individual and his community. The educational system must feed on the values of its culture. In return, the social environment becomes fertile and becomes ready for development. The media plays an important role as well. It has a dangerous effect on people when it becomes a tool of destruction and shallowness.[81]

This is why we must rethink and review our educational systems. But before we do this we must also find qualified teachers who can prove themselves with the result of success they achieve every year. This would show how far they motivated their students and to what extent they planted within them the ecstasy and joy of faith.

In this framework, Gülen proposes a role model for the successful school. In this way, he planted the contemporary Turkish schools which gained the approval of the society before the approval of the government. The movement of opening schools inside and outside Turkey has a goal of producing successful students who can excel and become the seeds of prosperity in their societies. Through them life and civilization will be revived.

Gülen's school is characterized by scientific methodology and its goal, besides learning the sciences, is to become the medium for development and awakening the conscience and establishing spiritual and humanitarian ties.

In Gülen's philosophy, the highest goals of education are harmonizing and bringing together Muslims spiritually. The common history and the common religion demand harmonizing the educational systems together to bring the different countries of the *ummah* closer. This can occur by integrating the pedagogical systems and how we raise the youth for the project of serving their nation. This will achieve Islamic unity on many levels which can empower Muslims and provide them with dignity.

Certainly, the contemporary educational system is affected by the universal trend of creating dependency, which has affected the spiri-

---

[81]   Ibid., p. 27.

tual intuition which connects the individual with his origin. Contemporary schools along with the media succeeded in turning people away from their spiritual nature and made them become accustomed to cultures different from our Islamic culture. That new culture does not observe decency and does not care for religion. As a result, the present day Muslim has turned away from the original values. This turning away was associated with a rough attitude and emotional void which affected family unity and the ordinary intimate connection with people.

The efficient constructive pedagogies, which Gülen emphasizes, seek to instill the spirit of true faith and provide the nectar of sincerity within the souls of the youth. They receive it accompanied with cultural preparation and masterful knowledge in a way that the youth can taste it even while learning grammar, mathematics, algebra and finance and can find it in the examples and the conclusions drawn. In this sense, deep passion for the truth and love for knowledge can be generated within their hearts. They become honest and sincere in life; for life itself becomes an open book for the Hereafter which does not open without a guiding consciousness and consideration of the unseen.

The Most Important Pursuit of the Successful School

Intellectual pursuit remains the most important goal of the successful school. It focuses on filling the heart with love and fertilizing it with spiritual passion. It also prepares the intellectual faculty and energizes it to reach its full capacity. It allows the spirit of critical thinking and creativity to grow. Thus, the graduate takes this spirit from the school to any organization, adding to its assets a distinctive vitality which enriches life. Raising a new generation to think productively and objectively enables them to get used to connecting their minds with the universal pasture with all the meanings and clarification it contains. This is the ultimate goal for Gülen's school as he says, "The most effective aspect of raising the current generation is to ease their way to transform internally and connect to the realities of existence which motivates and strengthens rational thinking. Faith can be made lovable to them through an educational system that allows them to examine and think and train them to read the signs on the horizons and within the souls as if they were open books."[82]

There is no doubt that when the graduate ascends within his initial stages in a pedagogical, scientific and spiritual atmosphere he will be highly qualified, well-rounded and balanced to merge in practical life effectively, transforming the society by his humanitarian and pious character through which goodness and tolerance can flow.

This successful experience, which Gülen's movement seeks to extend to other areas, is accomplishing its goals at a steady pace wherever it goes. This is due to its ability to raise distinctive youth and prepare conscientious young adults who will play the leading role in constructing the future. It is the pillar upon which a brilliant horizon can be established.[83]

It is the duty of the living organism to take care of the youth and to look at his talents and abilities so that energies would not be wasted as is the case of our contemporary educational systems.

If there are no practical institutes and empowering programs that can receive the graduates and transform them into workers and men who are capable of progressing then the educational system is useless and pointless.

The shortcoming of our civil society in contributing to the constructive movement is the cause of the loss of energy and the waste of efforts especially considering there are many graduates every year who look for jobs and who keep cramming into a marketplace that is not open for them. These youth find themselves facing a dead-end road.

A true financial, cultural and productive investment must open the doors for the youth and integrate them into everyday life by preparing for them projects, jobs and finding channels for them to use their talents. This must be done in an ethical, enlightening atmosphere that empowers the wheel of production. This can contribute to the transformation of the society and reform it through following a straight doctrine that is governed by good values, pure goodness and tranquility.

---

[82] Ibid., p. 8.
[83] Ibid., pp. 21–35.

Culture and Structure

According to Gülen, a good environment has an essential role in building a balanced personality that is well connected with its origins; for it is the natural school which none escapes its effect. "Culture is the source of values in all civilizations. Culture is what prevails in social life which is the general atmosphere which embraces the *ummah* emotionally. It shapes its intellectual activity and enriches it. Thus, the relationship between the school and the culture is a natural interaction. As much as the school is directed towards the goal and is characterized by depth it becomes like the airport or the harbor from which the whole nation can take off from on the condition that it continues to integrate its gains into the pot that contains the essence of its culture."[84]

To construct, means to give birth to talents and genius. This is because it motivates the individual and the collective potential. It helps people to discover their talents and save them from being lost as often happens in many cultures. "The extraordinary success which was achieved in the past and today and the major global developments are tied to the genius of individuals and their different gifts. Social structure must give birth to brilliant inventors and the whole atmosphere must embrace the genius."[85] "A pious circle, which makes an effective atmosphere, is different from a dead atmosphere in the sense that it becomes like a fertile land that is ready for cultivation."[86]

Today, there are many schools that pretend to be civilized but in reality they need a full revision of their programs and goals. This type of school usually has no defined goal and at the most its function is to eliminate illiteracy. It keeps many youth from learning the profession they will work in early enough. There is no actual training for them in school and they may drop out of school and just learn something by themselves or find simple jobs. Even those who earn a degree find themselves in need of further practical training to be able to work. There is a huge gap today between the classical educational systems and the

---

[84] Ibid., pp. 26–27.
[85] Ibid., p.15
[86] Ibid.

fast developing information tools such as virtual media, computers, Internet, future sciences and their practical uses.

In today's world we have to renew our perspective of how a school should be and understand what is necessary to have an effective educational system that trains the students in these fields. The bankruptcy of the educational system in the medieval era caused the deterioration of the Islamic civilization. There is no doubt that the main factor that causes the deterioration in a civilization is the lack of perspective in the educational system and the absence of having a vision of the future which any educational system must have an insight about.

Gülen explains that the matrix of Sufi lodges, retreat centers and mosques continued to offer a kind of education that was cut off from real life and that has no aim and did not address the needs of the individuals and communities and did not pay attention to the deterioration that occurred to the *ummah*. This deepened the stagnation and blocked the horizon. It is natural for religious scholars that were raised in this atmosphere to only be able to teach the students how to memorize supplications as if this alone could change the crisis. They were heedless of the Guardian Protector's saying, "*And prepare against them whatever you are able of power and of steeds of war*" (al-Anfal 8:60).

Gülen points to that disastrous shortage in the traditional schools in the medieval era and explained how our cultural organizations in the past did not train the developing abilities within our intellects and the working capacities within our souls. They did not establish projects that could help the generations master their futures.

Gülen sees that this disastrous situation is still continuing. Our condition today concerning preparing our generations for the future is similar to their condition. They were heedless of the future and passive and we too are still asleep and have not been producing a schedule for any major and comprehensive projects that we strive to achieve in order to close the book of deterioration forever and attain salvation.[87]

---

[87] Ibid., p. 24.

The Keyword

In answering a question proposed to Gülen concerning how can faith transform the human being into a well-rounded (*kamil*) being, he answered, "The keyword is: There is no deity except Allah (*La ilaha illa Allah*)." It is the seed of faith and faith is the source of refining the souls' feelings. Faith encourages the souls to seek knowledge and to learn the science of the purification of the heart. It is an internal sense and is a towering figure that stretches its hands around the being. It surrounds the personality from all directions and this makes the person's behavior like that of a passionate longing lover. Faith deepens the essence of inner rituals which is God consciousness and conscience. Faith strengthens the person's connection with heaven and this causes his pursuit, his contribution and his production to gradually ascend to excellence, to benevolence and to sound rationality.

Faith purifies one's intention and holds him accountable before Allah and he acts only for His sake, pushed by what Gülen calls "The Central Attraction." The faithful's actions, behavior, pursuits and service are born from the direct taste of the refined essence that transcends all types of weaknesses through its spiritual nature. Thus, all of his achievements are characterized by beauty as a result of the deep penetrating love within him. The soul that is watered by faith leaves its mark on all actions, especially because his actions are characterized by accuracy, delicacy, and mastery as if they belong to the realm of art and culture.

The heart's motive directs all the responsible individual's actions and behavior. His pure motive covers his actions and manners with the love that overflows from his heart. For each effort he makes, his intention is to come close to Allah. Whatever is done for Allah must be accurate and elegant. This is why the faithful's actions are characterized by beauty and are close to excellence and perfection. The call of faith has the loudest voice no matter where the faithful, the man of heart, goes. Wherever he walks he hears its voice calling him to the true meaning of being a humanitarian and to the true meaning of the universe. He therefore hears Allah and transforms within the soul an emotional support which is reflected in having a vision for the future, having refined feelings and effective actions.[88]

Faith-based thought continues to influence all the theoretical and practical aspects and all that the spiritual person attaches his heart and energy to. This is because this thought is mixed with the invisible light which softens the being of the individual and transforms it and makes it attain a transparent nature. As the light becomes firmly established it becomes the natural image of the human being.[89] When that second nature grows within the individuals, the communities, the leaders and the societies who are in the labs, in the factories and in the workshops, it leads to firmly established activism that opens the door for building the civilization.

---

[88] Ibid., p. 51.
[89] Ibid., p. 52.

Chapter Four

Fethullah Gülen and the Philosophy of Construction without Violence

F
ethullah Gülen, the advocate of faith, founded the faith-based advocacy service and opened it to a new vital horizon. He gave it the nature of renaissance that suits the spirit of the current era. He emerged victorious after a bitter struggle. He earned people's acknowledgement and he even earned the respect of the opponents who were forced to acknowledge his efforts after his service was established everywhere across Turkey and many other Islamic countries. His extended efforts reached across the continents and it is still growing with the dynamic self-immanent movement which he founded and follows up on. His groups have been multiplying in a steady blessed pace and they cover many educational and cultural fields and social and diverse preparatory organizations, in addition to the emissary works and the spread of peace.

Gülen's doctrine can be considered a philosophy that has opened many constructive initiatives. Gülen turned to his country's history and was inspired by the virtuous Ottoman taking into consideration their many completed achievements and their partly completed achievements and sensing the hopes of many generations and the wishes of many pious reformers. Thus, he started the construction adding what his genius guided him to add, inspired by the epiphanies and the visions of the renaissance. He kicked off the start and sewed the fabric of civilization by establishing enlightened communities through serving the needs and connecting networks that are specialized in diverse fields.

In this way, he opened the path in the face of goodwill efforts to begin a blessed era of giving, of becoming fruitful and benevolent.

Gülen facilitated the conditions that attracted throngs of fortunate people who were ready for activism. They knew the essence of true existence and tasted the nectar which emerges from service and is produced by exerting one' efforts and wealth for the sake of Allah. Gülen has paved a way upon which the rich can walk and record their names among the pious people who choose to invest in a fruitful field. They lend Allah a beautiful loan and He multiplies it for them.

The least that we can point to concerning Gülen's achievements is that he ended his struggle by empowering people who had submitted their weapons and surrendered to the deteriorating tendencies. His opponents could no longer deceive people and convince them of their confused policies.

From the darkness of apostasy and alienation, Gülen emerged as an advocate and a clarifier who shows the way to the people who are ready to serve and to advocate the call of Allah. He paved the road for them and they walked towards renaissance which gave birth to many spiritual lodges, social organizations, and enlightened groups that can establish the edifice of faith on their land once again and walk towards globalization.

Many benevolent people were chained by confusing ideologies which blocked the road in their faces and prevented them from contributing in the construction of civilization under the claim that religion opposes progress. This was the cause of the underdevelopment.

The most important motive that pushed the opponents to exclude the faithful from the circle is their certainty that the abilities of the faithful are incomparable. The one who disciplines the self by obeying Allah and is filled with love for Allah and His Messenger, and who lives in a modest way and gives for the sake of Allah is not the same as the one who lives in spiritual confusion, who submits to his selfish whims and becomes incapacitated to lead or to form a strategic plan for the *ummah* to walk towards the renaissance.

Many years have passed and we are riding with the confused who had gone astray. This led to destruction and ruined the *ummah* and we stood bankrupt at the doors. Humanitarian values eroded in the society and nobility left us after it was the characteristic of perfection and chivalry. After we deviated from the straight way they adorned for us non-religion disregarding that our creed was the foundation of our excellence. But we became ill, polarized by the nations around us.

This was confronted by Gülen's achievements and his great actions and new openings and he defeated the forces of confusion, while many who used to hold onto the tenets of Islam, but who were far astray from it, shrank.

This is glad tidings which opens the field before all Muslims. It removes many obstacles which the authoritarian regimes established as they blindly followed the West, walking in the opposite direction to history and turning away from the sacred message which Islam entrusted to us and which formed us and became the lights that direct our attachments and our natural belonging.

We can say that today we are keeping pace with the Arab Spring,[90] transforming from the reactive apologetic stage and the state of being held under oppression and corruption, to the vast state of activism and involvement in the political arena without any obstacle. But if we are not qualified and ready to construct our civilization, it will be a danger that threatens the credibility of our struggle and the political gains which we earned through effort and great endeavor.

There is nothing worse for the Islamic movements than gaining the flag of leadership from the people in these countries where the revolutions of the youth have taken place and then failing, may Allah forbid, to deliver and being unable to lead people on the road of faith and failing to construct a complete civil model that can attract the attention of people everywhere.

Every accomplishment in the civil field which Muslims achieve can become a symbol and earn global recognition that can show people the reality of Islam. The world has become like one village and our Islamic countries are no more than an organism in this big village. Thus, every constructive achievement in our area will attract the travelers and can illuminate their curiosity to want to know the source of our virtues.

---

[90] Which we hope will not become a disappointment.

Founding the Movement for the Contemporary Renaissance

Since his youth, Gülen has continued to sculpt the stones and to level pathways with his fingertips for the *ummah* to emerge from the depth of the darkness in which it fell. Gülen has prepared the wings, initiated the tools, and established the organizations that are charged to serve.

From his tower he follows the flow and leads the battle of spiritual and material construction. He guides the right wing and the left wing and he strengthens the foremost runners. He moves the servants to support the heart whenever a gap appears or a disturbance occurs.

On the same ground where the conqueror liberated people from the darkness of lethargy and crossed its sea towards Europe, Gülen stood firm and succeeded in opening fields of faith-based services. He spread his message in the world. His march is like that of Alexander the Great or the march of Dhu'l-Qarnayn (The Man of the Two Centuries).[91] His march starts from the intermediate realm carrying the torch of pure goodness, not to invade or to accomplish selfish and perishable success but to establish the Divine Word around the world in order to establish a civilized Islamic renaissance in order to resume the leadership which was lost centuries ago.

It is a march following the footsteps of Abu Ayub al-Ansari and those who followed him carrying the flag of light to the corners of the earth. Every opening essay for a newspaper and every media announcement of service and every lecture he delivers for the devoted and every chapter in a book which Gülen issues is a hermeneutic message that is full of the incoming epiphanies which this devout man receives and lives through the passing days and weeks which he spends in retreat.

Gülen's daily schedule follows the rhythm of: "When you are empty then get filled—and to your lord direct your full desire."[92] This is what

---

[91] It can also be translated as the Man of the Two Horns.

[92] Gülen says, "In reality true love starts with that step. If we discuss the intuitive love of the human being for his parents, wife and children, etc. that love should be in the framework which Allah demands. Otherwise, Allah would bring trials in this world of many kinds to reckon or He may postpone the reckoning till the Day of

he recommends for all the workers in the faith-based services; for they have to follow the Qur'anic guidance which established the daily schedule for the Muslim, dividing it between work and worship.

There is no rest for the devout man and he does not have family or home. He fully immerses himself in carrying the great responsibility to meet the chances of fate. He cannot bear to have a competitor who can be ahead of him in the race to love. This is because the love of family and of belongings can soon turn to a trial that can become an obstacle for devotion and giving one's heart to the cause.

He continues to trickle drops of gold from a celibate spirit which is completely attached to the prayer niche for Divine provision, and battles lethargy and passivity in all directions.

The appearance of a devout leader in the *ummah* is a Divine Gift of generosity and a great fortune given to people. This is because lining up behind the devout leaders has a guaranteed success, a blessed outcome and a fruitful result and it is never disappointing. This is because faith makes those who line up behind the devout leader certain from the very beginning in the later reward and they focus on that aspect to strengthen their resoluteness. Thus, they become tranquil about the efforts they exert and recognize that even if they do not gain the practical expectations and witness the fruits of what they plant, they still have the confidence in earning the reward of the Generous Care Giver. Thus, their expectations are for the Hereafter and Allah alone becomes enough for them.

The Role of the Erudite in the Renaissance

After Western colonization, we inherited a passive attitude towards our heritage and culture. This colonization caused us to adopt Western values and traditions and our elites became uprooted from their origin. Everything had to meet the Western standards and people started

---

Judgment. In brief, the faithful person is a balanced human being and he must maintain that balance at all times and protect it from the influence of the society and from his lower desires and selfish whims." From Gülen's book *Adwa'u Qur'aniyyah fi Sama' al-Wijdan* (Qur'anic Lights in the Heavens of Conscience), p.78.

to imitate and copy the West because they admired its advancement. People thought that mere imitation would achieve a renaissance, forgetting that regimes and cultures have to emerge from their own soil and cannot be rooted in foreign soil. The democracy which caused the West to enjoy internal peace and global admiration has lately started to show another side. The political parties are controlled by hidden forces and lobbies that seek their own self-interests and they support certain nominees to win an election not based on his ability to serve the country and people but because he would support their own interests. They deceive people with campaigns and debates under the slogan of freedom and fair competition. Democracy today is controlled by money, media, art, and commercial interests. These universal forces make up ideologies to serve their interests everywhere. This has become very clear in the political field of today.

Decades may pass while we are trying to learn democracy from the West and when we master it we will find the West has moved to another stage. We would even fake democracy just to resemble the West. Years and different stages may pass while we are trying to build our civilization by copying other people's values and systems. We cannot see how the people in the West are swayed and how they are shifting their values because they realize how they have deviated from the truth. Today, the West is trying to renew its vitality but because the page is turned,[93] the West cannot return to the same spirit until it is directed towards humanitarian values and unless it abandons idolizing their way and going further astray.

The Muslim nation is required to initiate a global renaissance again.[94] We can establish systems that follow the spirit of the Divine law which is based upon having reverence for and faith in Allah. This is a central pillar in any hope for a true opening that can take humanity towards hopeful happiness. The fear of Allah is the cornerstone upon which all

---

[93] *"There is a term written for everything"* (ar-Ra'd 13:38).

[94] Gülen says, "After the unfortunate halt, our world can once again move the spirits and the enlightened ones to achieve the second or the third global renaissance." *Wa Nahnu Nabni Hadaratina* (As We Are Building Our Civilization), p. 30.

matters can be balanced and it guarantees goodness for all people and guarantees perfection, justice and brotherhood among all people.

There is no doubt that Gülen looks at these horizons which are opened now and which we cannot see because we have given up on the renaissance. But Gülen believes that now it is the Prophet's nation's time to take off; for this is the universal law of the changing aspects of civilizations. We are calling for prayer and people are listening to us more than before. Thus, we must start establishing the second renaissance.

We must take the reign of the renaissance to direct it towards the right path in accordance to the oath we gave to Allah by looking at our qualifications and the universality of the message of Islam which we were honored with. Islam will remain the force of reviving the right civilization at all times. Islam will continue to be the source of the leaps we take until the train settles at its station. By the favor of this creed no lethargy can stop us. No matter how long it takes we can stand up again and renew our steadfastness; for we are like the owner of fire who is never deprived of the source of energy.

When the engine turns and the flow spreads, all efforts must join. We must join our hands and hearts and focus on reviving that which will save us from failure.

The Arab elites have an obligation to strengthen the ties of unity among all the Muslim nations and especially with Turkey considering its new auspicious direction. We must strengthen rapprochement to achieve true merging. Merging would not harm us because we have a sound perspective. We should achieve rapprochement with Turkey, even in case it joins the EU, because any advancement in one country will advance the rest of the *ummah* and strengthen it spiritually.

We have to take a good lesson from the West that is being swayed from financial competition and promote diversity within unity. Each success that one country achieves, the West utilizes that success for their mutual success. Nonetheless, we see them facing economic difficulties and unemployment that makes them focus on the indigenous and spend millions of euros to save the countries that were torn apart by a large deficit and could not achieve their plans.

The responsibility of the Arab erudite is to help the Muslim nations cross the obstacles of separateness, fear and the ethnic and tribal tendencies and overcome past problems and historical faults. We must take the West as a role model considering the spirit by which it overcame the results of destructive wars. Germany and France are in natural unity today which strategic and mutual benefits demand. Separateness results in weakness and the loss of a global position. Their unity guarantees for them a fence that protects them from competitive countries in the east and in the south.

We have inherited a naïve confidence and a blind creed in the idealism of the Western regimes and we followed their system and we became frozen. As a result we were overtaken by ethnic differences and separateness. Before, the *ummah* was one even at the times when there were disputes and when it was ruled by dynasties that competed among themselves to rule. Nonetheless, people, interactions, and the deep feeling of unity and open borders allowed the exchange among the *ummah*'s scholars, merchants, students and experts. Mutual interaction which was based on the oneness of beliefs and on certainty in the common fate remained. The Arabic language continued on the tongues of Muslims everywhere. This assured a feeling of unity. All pressures and necessities demand that today the Qur'an and the Arabic language should be the factors that should unite all Muslim nations. History will not forgive how we recklessly let go of it.

The cruel extortion which we face today and our acceptance to play the role of the prey as we face oppressive capitalism demands of us to hasten our work and to be resolute in saving ourselves from the canines of capitalism. The flow of oil makes some nations unaware of what is happening to other Muslim nations today. The oil wealth should not go to waste before the whole nation benefits from it to achieve its renaissance so that we can be a nation that stands on its feet.

The call for rapprochement and merging which Gülen adopts, makes many forces within our nation fear him because his call does not serve their interests. The intellectuals, the politicians, the researchers and artists of our nations should busy themselves with explaining the mutual benefit of rapprochement and unity.

To stir ethnic and racist dust must be forgotten and objections raised against merging and mutual planning must be refuted. These objections usually come from short-sighted people who seek to isolate their countries and deceive their people for the sake of their selfish interests.

Globalization demands us to design a pedagogical system and a functional media that can form the cornerstone to teach people and the youth in all countries. And also motivate them to work hard in order to achieve rapprochement and natural ties with Muslim nations to protect our position and guarantee the means for survival.

Nationalism does not mean to abrogate strategic unity with the stronger brother nor does it mean not to give a helping hand to the weaker one. Today, we see Europe wiping out large debts for Greece in order to strengthen the unity of the people on the old continent.

Nonetheless, we still listen to poisoning speeches that have no vision and claim that the rapprochement between Turkey and the Arab world is a plan that hides motives of reviving the old "Khilafah." But today, the West is constructing its own Khilafah and it goes to far ends to tighten its unity. This is because they see that unity is the formidable dam that can protect its prosperity and global status.

To dream of the return of the Khilafah cannot come true because history does not go backward and because today's circumstances are different from the past. The *ummah*'s dream is to form a unity within which diversity is maintained. This is the way that can assure its dignity no matter what name that unity is given. This is a revolutionary dream within the heart of every Muslim in all enlightened circles.

The erudite writes for people and in many cases his understanding of people's dreams is lacking. His perspective cannot reach the epiphanies that can descend as illuminating light awakening people's consciences and motivating them to change. The greatest focus of this intellectual is to examine the status quo and emotionally share the stagnation that his people feel. In this way, he only shares the general and common complaint and the bitter confusion which fills the atmosphere. He only goes with the flow of all people and expresses their emotions. His spirit translates the sense of defeat and he cries out as the voice of people's pain and sorrows. He settles in the emotional state and his popularity stems from it. He is like the crying moaning voice that we hear at funerals and memorials.

The intellectual writes in the name of the *ummah* and with its spirit and emotions. He goes deep into its living states, pains and sorrows and his breath exhales the words from a burnt heart. It is not enough for him to do so on occasions or when he is delivering a speech or standing on a platform but he immerses his whole life and devotes his years to battling hellfire. This is why his moaning is exhibited in every letter he utters and every phrase he forms. His words melt with his heart and in this way he makes himself the torch that is kindled to illuminate the path for the *ummah* and to show it the paved road from which it can find life.

There are only a few revered intellectuals like that. In fact they are rare to find. They are kept behind veils hidden from people but because of their genuine principles, they will eventually succeed in overcoming the siege set in front of them and they will pierce to the heart of the scene, attracting people who will follow them individually, in groups, throngs and nations, and they will eventually fulfill what Allah promised the pious to achieve.

To repeat the supplication after such master guides and to support them in what they do with all means, sacrifices and generous giving is the way to achieve the renaissance. To be close to them, to supplicate Allah on their behalf and to join their efforts verbally and by participating in their campaigns will strengthen the call for the revolutionary awakening which they summon people for. People get emotionally attached to them and they walk with them and behind them towards achieving great goals. This effort is rewarding because the one who exerts effort for it, is one who responds to the caller for pure goodness.

The Strategy of Non-Violence

The main characteristic of Gülen's call is to avoid violent confrontations and its opposition to rigid and harsh tendencies in doctrine and in life. Gülen's call is a peaceful, stoical and balanced call which cares for investing in good deeds and not in wasting one's time, chances and talents, but for using everything to serve the call and to spread its pro-grams. His call is dedicated to watching its step, affirming its standing, having insightful projects, and forming practical services.

Gülen sees Islam as the Divine religion which cannot be obstruct-ed by a time limit because there is no particular time set for it to spread and there is no particular period in which it is going to spread across the earth. It is not a religion tied by a particular generation that has to spread it across the world. Islam is a doctrine which the Divine Will prepared for all of humanity. It is Allah's natural way that spiri-tual guidance attracts people when their feelings of being lost are greater and when their needs increase and when they lose sight of their possibilities. Only then will they start to look everywhere for a savior or a voice that shows them the way of salvation. They may be deceived by mirages for a period of time but they soon discover that these mirages are shadows that have no realities and they seek refuge in heaven. They then accept the Divine law and respond to Allah's Call.

Islam has settled within all the lands in which it has entered, after people tasted its nectar. People found out that Islam is the highest ideal with lofty ethics and values which people's innate nature like and which are intuitively preferred. This is why people continue to glorify their religion. Therefore, all situations and stages, no matter how hard they are, will just increase the piercing of Islam into the depth of the souls as it continues to awaken people's consciences.

The defeats, regressions and hardships of the Muslim people for centuries have made them realize that they deviated from Islam and this realization exists within all levels and backgrounds. Muslims real-ize that it all happened because they transgressed the limits set by Islam for the foundation of civilization and happiness. Muslims hold themselves responsible for their lethargy and sitting on the sidelines incapacitated and losing their dignity. They realize that it was Islam that gave them their glorious history and that by returning to it they will return to the right path which fate has prepared them for considering that they are the *ummah* which emerged with goodness for all people, enjoining what is known to common reason and our innate nature and prohibiting what is rejected by common reason and our innate nature and to believe in Allah.

With this conviction Gülen prefers a calm and peaceful call over work that is based on fanatic enthusiasm that may soon be cut off or stopped. A steady slow progress is better than making a quick leap that is aimless. Righteousness in executing plans and programs can be strengthened and yield results when it is established in a progressive steady movement with successive performances that expand its field with time, tying different communities together.

These natural ties and diligent continuous effort complete the construction in a civilized doctrine which enriches the life of the individuals and the society following this verse of the Qur'an, "*And say: 'Work (righteousness) soon Allah will observe your work'*" (at-Tawbah 9:105).

Gülen's standard is to have a pure heart that can serve while feeling he is being watched by Allah in all that he does. According to him, this is the attitude that should guide us in our mission. We should have Allah as the Watcher before anyone else. Truly, Gülen sees that the heart must hold this belief in order to be devoted to service. To be sincere and honest in fulfilling one's duties and planning one's goals are essential for success. This spiritual characteristic is what helps us to devote ourselves and offer sacrifices like one in self-battle and all that he looks for is to attain triumph over his lower desires or to gain true existence (i.e. death of the ego).

To be steadfast and have insight concerning how to invite people to the path is to care for each particular situation. This means to care about serving the call inside one's country and outside one's country. Globalization, which claims to be opened to diversity, should not make us believe in that slogan if in reality there is restriction of spiritual activities and non-profit civil work. There are groups who want to see a world without any spiritual activities. They only want consumerism and want to earn what they can from industrial companies and big markets. We should not expect from globalization and its occupation of all the voices of the media by which it directs people to serve particular groups' interests to welcome any call for spiritual awakening. This is because spiritual awakening makes guiding man its first goal, and to refine his ethics and values by helping him to discipline his lower desires and whims, train him to make sound rational decisions, and enable him to resist the ideology of consumerism. Spirituality empowers the human being to reject his animalistic tendencies, which are accepted under the claim of false freedom and calls for indulgence in materialistic pleasures.

To stimulate man's lower desires and consumer tendencies is a cunning plot which capitalism endorses through monopolies and what particular global corporations use to tempt people. This is the new soft occupation that has replaced past military occupation. This type of occupation is more dangerous for it bends the necks and strips people of their immunity so that they give away their identities, their system of values and that which constitutes their unity.

The role of the media that was globalized to cross all boundaries is to ridicule everything sacred except material wealth and it focuses only on how to earn wealth and how to spend it. The media transgresses the limit of training people to obey and pushes them to blindly follow ribaldries and lewdness. The most dangerous effects of the contemporary media is taming the human being, enslaving people, and influencing them negatively. The media has become a global addiction[95] and people cannot escape from its authoritative way.

People submitted to the media to the degree that they sleep and wake up watching its mesmerizing material that destroys all values. Many meaningless cartoons and other vain movies lower the intellectual activities of man and make him oblivious. This visual and audible culture which people are used to is destructive to the soul. It has made man lose his dignity and honor and accept profanity and the shrinking of the gap between him and animals, letting his lower desires control him and indulging in violence and pornography.

---

[95] We predict the liberation of man from the grasp of the visual and audio media which besieges him today and fills his life with its material. The future of the movie industry will be similar to the Greek and Roman dramas which history turned the page on and which we now look at as ancient. Humanity might transgress the limits, lose its balance and pass through different stages, but that will not last long. What we are concerned about today is people's addiction to the low quality Hollywood movies.

Today, many people spend their time watching TV going from one channel to another all day long. This is what the marketing industry gets people addicted to. This disempowers the human being and makes him more of an unconscious follower.

On the other hand, Islam invites man to sit in the circles of Divine remembrance which can make him feel peaceful, tranquil and more contemplative as he listens to the Holy Qur'an recited rhythmically. The peacefulness, the tranquility and the contemplative mood stays with him even after he leaves the prayers. If he increases his prayer by performing night vigils and waking up at dawn to pray then he would feel harmonious with his innate nature and he would carry that feeling with him all day long. This can empower man emotionally and spiritually and strengthen his vitality and steadfastness. This is contrary to the culture of consumerism, with its dangerous drama which grips us, increases our desires and leaves us unsatisfied.

There is goodness in silence and abandoning vain talks which is a universal virtue that many cultures around the world embrace and which have been affected by the media. The contemporary media has made man talkative and lessens his listening ability. Being bombarded by visual images all the time consumes his ability to think and to feel and it wastes most of his time which he could better use in more beneficial activities that would have more lasting effects. Today, surfing the web keeps one busy and deprives man of feeling the joy of being fulfilled by direct contact and interaction with others.

Gülen sees that moderation is an important characteristic which enables man to build a hopeful civilization. Modesty can also extend to include talking. Indulging in physical pleasure is not the only activity that can be out of balance, but talking can also have a wasteful nature and the ability to strip the human being of his values and rationality. Talking can also be a lower form of satiety because it can lower one's capacity for refinement and to have sound reason and chivalry. Vain talk is part of the lower desires that can corrupt one's conscience. It is the result of the culture of contemporary materialism which targets our spiritual and loftier nature which the human being revered throughout the ages.

There is no wonder then that the Qur'an explains to us the benefit of silence which many purified people, such as Mary and Zechariah and many others practiced and sought refuge in their way of communicating with Allah. In Islam, spiritual retreat is based on silence and the only speech allowed is supplications and Qur'an recitation. These spiritual retreats are what prepare man to change the course of history.

The goal of capitalism that has monopolies is to make the earth a supermarket and to turn all people into consumers who are hungry for goodies. This is why they see danger in Islam; for the spirituality of religion refines the human being and enables him to be moderate and balanced and not to be easily stimulated by worldly advertisements.

In the contemporary materialistic civilization, man is accustomed to advertising which causes man to lose his innate humanity; for he misses the spiritual aspect which can keep him moderate and balanced. By destroying the great nature of man and causing the death of his spirit he turns into a consuming beast governed by cruelty and lower desires and is subjugated to the materialistic nature of modernity. Even sport has lost its noble character and turned into competitive, violent, deceptive, rough and cruel activities. Even the symbols of beauty, that have always been an aspect of sport, have disappeared. Sport today pushes people to extremes, depriving them of their values. Women have entered the field of cruel competition and they are pushed to extremes and to abandon their values and their delicate nature.

Today, the voice of reason calls for moderating the material development by following the rules of balance and moderation and accepting our innate nature to put a limit to this rejection of religion. It is that rejection that caused man to become overly materialistic and subjugated him to the physical body.

Gülen continues to call individuals and communities to be balanced and be modest and moderate and to have mastery over one's whims in order to return the soul to its vitality, the intellect to its luminosity and rationality to its soundness. In this way, contemporary man can transcend the trap of fleeting pleasures and avoid falling into the abyss of bottomless vulgarity.

Choosing the Parties That Are Ready for Dialogue

The civilized initiative for dialogue which Gülen proposes is a must. It is the way of the noble Messenger who initiated dialogues with people, including the Sultans of all global powers in his era. He established a good association with the Ethiopian King. This was because the noble Messenger realized that the King could have a great role in spreading the message and attracting diverse parties to converse with each other, which would gain sympathy and respect for his cause.

In the way the Prophet talked with an-Najashi, Gülen found an example of how to address his soul from the perspective of his creed. He spoke with him about Mary and Jesus Christ, peace be upon both of them. The Prophetic doctrine shows us how we should converse with people of other religions and share with them what we have in common with their creed and book.[96] The noble communication the Prophet had with an-Najashi manifests the universality of the Islamic message. This should be the role model of the *ummah* and how it can spread the Islamic message to the world.

The Arabian Peninsula witnessed the Prophet's followers as they migrated to Ethiopia and how the Ethiopian King was hospitable to them. This was seen as a threat. Thus, they did not hesitate to try to disrupt that connection; for they saw it as a successful step in the Prophet's favor. Many tribes started to reconsider their firm convictions and opened up to explore the new religion. In this way, many Arab tribes became ready to enter the religion of Allah in throngs. The Prophet's good relation with the Ethiopian King played a great role in affecting people and his move was fruitful. He could have directed the early Muslim emigrants to go to the countries that were under the rule of the Roman Church, but he saw that Africa was more ready to have a dialogue. Thus, he sent the first group of emigrants to Ethiopia.

Many African countries such as Egypt, Ethiopia, Libya, and Numidia were opened to the spiritual call and they were close to the Arabs considering their spiritual perspective of the universe. The Oriental

---

[96] Gülen, *Adwa'u Qur'aniyyah fi Sama' al-Wijdan* (Qur'anic Lights in the Heavens of Conscience), p. 163.

atmosphere was deeply rooted in these countries more than others. This is why the Prophet's relation with Ethiopia was fruitful and caused the required echo.

Nonetheless, the Messenger did not exempt any ruler in his era with whom he had not tried to communicate with. He tried to build a living bridge with Africa. One of the fruits he gained from his effort was his positive communication with Egypt which resulted in his marriage to Maria, the Coptic.

Following this doctrine, Gülen emphasizes the importance of opening dialogues with those who are ready for it. We must converse with each group in a way that suits its culture and its level of civility. If the one who participates in a dialogue has no knowledge of the rules of dialogues and does not follow a constructive way of communication, he would usually end up being disappointed and would not attract any attention. On the contrary, ignorance of the etiquette of dialogue would often result in repulsing people away from Islam and away from Muslims. This is what we witness today. Many Muslim emigrants and their irresponsible behavior and ignorant attitudes towards others repulse others. They live isolated and go to extremes even in the way they dress, which is only a display of their shallowness and primitive attitude.

The Muslim should instead seek to be a good example to call people to Islam and use appropriate and gradual means to educate others about Islam. It would be a great gain for the *ummah* if Muslims represented the beauty and peacefulness of Islam which would automatically close the door before the bigots who attack Islam.

The most effective way to serve Islam is to show a civil and sophisticated attitude and to show industrial progress to compete with other nations which Muslims have not yet achieved. Unfortunately, most Islamic countries are captives of lethargy. People can be inspired by the ideal representatives of Islam who can exemplify the meaningfulness of spirituality.

The call must spread a sense of security and tranquility in all the places it reaches, even within the Islamic society itself. Having a friendly attitude is an essential factor in all efforts of enlightening. Contemporary cultures have made the soul become rigid, biased and prejudiced. It decreased the tempo of sacredness and faith within people's consciences. It becomes difficult for the preacher to achieve his goal in illuminating people's consciences unless he considers the psychological effect of modernity and the wide spread bias, rigidity and prejudice. He must understand what inhabits the heart of the city he lives in and the type of hate or stereotype that people have, especially for Islam. He must be careful not to provoke hostility towards himself. He should be aware of the controversial issues and the provocative attitude that some Western ideologies have against Islam.

The distinct development that could be achieved by the desired civilization has a meaning and a core goal to show the efficacy of the ideal religion which meets the needs and hopes of man regardless of his time or place. Islam offers a refuge for man from falling into the faults that ruined many civilizations throughout the ages. It assures his freedom and opens for him a wide field to invest his inner abilities and to utilize them for pure goodness, to construct a civilization and fulfill his role as the Divine vicegerent on earth. When some philosophers in the West called for murdering god they actually killed the spirit of the human being. Saving humanity from this self-destructive fate can only be achieved at the hands of Muslims in accordance to the teachings of Islam.

To accomplish their role, some conditions have to be met first to establish the Islamic civilization. The *ummah* must work tirelessly to actualize its distinction and to defeat its lethargy. The Qur'an informed us about the dam which Dhu'l-Qarnayn built as a barrier between the possessors of faithful belief in the truth and those who reject the truth. Similarly, we must build a spiritual dam to protect us from the destructive wind until we meet the conditions and rise to protect others from the selfish ego and the evil of self-destruction, and deviation from the clear truth.

Chapter Five

The Significance of Action

Gülen says, "Ideas should be applied. Otherwise, they will remain mere fantasies."[97] Many times we have quoted Gülen speaking of realistic ideas. What we mean by "action" here is to witness the characteristic of reality and to physically detect its constitution and causes and then to visualize practical solutions for its challenges and obstacles.

Certainly, there are endless thoughts and ideas that emerge in every era and in every place that visualize solutions and offer alternatives to enhance the status quo of humanity and to lead it to a straight way. But most of these thoughts are short-sighted while others remain as theories only. Most thoughts cannot master the alchemy of cultures and civilizations which can direct them towards relief.

If we examine many of the contemporary intellectual writings we can see how they focus on abstracts and thus remain in the theoretical field and are based on speculations that have no control over life. These are mere metaphysical initiatives which many philosophers, ideologists and intellectuals are immersed in, following the path of the ancients. In this sense, they are mere echoes and a redundant copy of dreaming about the Virtuous City. Theories can take their adherents too far outside the realm of reality. Their theories are not objective even though they imagine that they are actively aware of the status quo and claim to establish the way of changing it.

---

[97] Gülen, *Wa Nahnu Nabni Hadaratina* (As We Are Building Our Civilization), p. 58.

What distinguishes Gülen's thought is that he effectively grasps the significance of action. He recognizes the important role which the Muslim intellectual should play in the era of failure which the *ummah* has been living in for the last two centuries. The intellectual's role is a rescuing role that focuses on pursuing goals without hesitation or delay, to awaken the *ummah* and restore its wellness.

According to Gülen, "action" has a condition, which is a free state in the theoretical plan for the renaissance of civilization. This is a practical way which requires a qualified faithful believer. The foundation of civilization is a free independent state and its most precious asset is time.[98]

This is an objective moderate perspective. Many opponents of authoritative regimes have revolution as their priority and openly call for the removal of these governments in order to achieve reform and start constructing the civilization. But Gülen, with his practical approach, sees that this state must be established upon the principle of freedom; for only a free state can be ready for major changes and taking leaps. Gülen is then a practical thinker whose thought is essentially inspired by the status quo and his direct connection with it. He realized that fortune and major transformations can be achieved at the hand of a guiding government that understands its role and executes it. This government with its two wings must embrace the constituents of the society and push the civilization to revival from within the people.

This practical approach seeks to shorten the time and effectively accomplish the goals. Indeed, Gülen sees man as the active agent who is always renewing his spirit and abilities to achieve the renaissance. Thus, it all starts by planning to find that active man and preparing him for the transformation. If this preparation is achieved under the care of the government, it would be faster and more inclusive contrary to the efforts and preparations that occur outside governmental supervision or in opposition to it; for in this case all efforts would be like swimming against the current. This usually results in opposition and repression which forms obstacles against any awakening. In fact, it can

---

[98] Ibid., p. 18.

destroy any awakening movement and force its decline or force it to work secretively which endangers many workers. This can limit the effect and the results of any awakening movement.

There are selfish motives which can be seen reflected in some preached slogans which rely on exclusive actions and systems. These groups make the group its goal and so they focus on forming factional entities or organizations more than they focus on service and real construction.

There is no doubt that political pressures and repressive regimes result in the formation of these secretive groups and they naturally form fractional organizations and hidden entities because their ability to freely move is limited and restricted and surrounded by threats. Their effect is slow and obstructed and this pushes them to be even more cautious and more determined to achieve the reform even on a smaller scale. They keep working secretly in hope of change and having better conditions.

This is why Gülen stresses the importance of having a nation that supports freedom in order to achieve the renaissance. A government that supports freedom can guarantee the renaissance and put it in the framework of a national project which everyone works for. In this way, the renaissance becomes the central pursuit which all efforts join in and all wills integrate to achieve and reap its blessings.

There is no doubt that entrusting the renaissance to governments that support freedom is Gülen's perspective which he formed based on his own life's experience and the difficult situations he faced having lived in a country that followed a policy of alienation that sought to imitate other cultures and completely abandon its original identity.

Advancing moral work requires a practical effective plan that motivates people to construct their civilization in the right way. This plan is progressing slowly under repressive and opposing regimes. Nonetheless, Gülen's deepest hopes kept moving him to devote his life to awaken people to finding their roots under a regime that subjected them to continual uprooting by persistently using all means available.

Gülen realized the importance of the few stones which he was placing for the awakening. He realized the value of the steps he was taking and the effort he was exerting towards spreading an awakening movement. He was certain that gaining even a tiny spot in the luminous land of the Divine Call is a great conquest.

The State, the Leader, the Individual and the Construction of Civilization

It is an essential role of the government to adopt the renaissance movement. Regimes and governments are not established but to exert their efforts and enlist their administrative and central executive branches and utilize their natural resources and the community's efforts to achieve construction and facilitate civil methodology to enhance life and allow the society to prosper. It is the government's function to make investments and to have the will to steadily progress towards prosperity and reform.

This can only occur when the government has mastered its affairs and its decisions and if it is free from all restrictions that may paralyze its movement and obstruct its will. This is why we see that Mr. Gülen emphasizes freedom as the condition that allows the government to earn the qualifications in order to achieve a renaissance and facilitate the way for it.

The free nation is a nation that can make its own plans, illustrate its path and direct itself strategically in a way that allows it to avoid falling into the traps of any powerful interest groups that seek to exploit it. These powerful groups use monopolies to keep resources and benefits in their control. At the same time, they manipulate weak nations to keep them in the abyss of dependency and lethargy.

Gülen brings attention to the fact that when the leaders and policies fail to govern the nations to the right way and fail to have a vision, they cause their citizens to suffer and deepen the lethargy of the nation and weaken its status among other nations.

Surely, happiness depends on the leaders! When a leader, who bases his choices on sound insight and makes rational decisions and strengthens his nation emerges, the whole nation walks with steady steps, determination and a clear vision towards achieving its goal of constructing civilization.

According to Gülen, the emergence of intellectual leaders who have sound reason is the best tool to prepare the vehicle which can drive the society towards salvation. Having a good leader is the best fortune which nations and countries should aspire to have.

A resolute regime can shorten the distance to civilization. This is because it completely throws itself into achieving its goals. It stirs the spirit of enthusiasm in its people and trains them to master their work and strengthen their determination, wisdom and shrewdness which can guarantee success.[99]

The wise regime is one that carries its responsibility in raising man and opening opportunities for him. It should work tirelessly to create opportunities which guide the entire society towards a solid structure. One of the best qualities a wise regime can have is how to utilize time and invest in it because wasting time is the main symptom of lethargy and being far from the right way and from success.

In all states, the responsibility and the role of the elites are very important factors in kindling the torch of awakening. Many times, the torch was lit by individuals; for the good examples of spiritual and intellectual leaders is the flame which fate utilizes to revive life and to renew the rise of dawn.

Building equipment that produces the elites and multiplies them in number is the seed that the enlightened ones achieve with their tireless efforts and persistence. Good people with souls that love giving and righteousness are attracted to them. What attracts them to the leader is his piousness and devotion to serve good causes. Every group gathers to achieve good work and their giving becomes fruitful. The galaxy is no more than a collection of brilliant stars gathering in the loftiest space circulating around suns and moons supplied with light, order, motion and functions!

---

[99]   Review what Gülen wrote about "the state" and the proper characteristics that it should have to carry its historical and civil responsibilities in his book *Wa Nahnu Nuqimu Sarh ar-Ruh* (As We Are Erecting the Edifice of Our Spirit), p. 102.

In this way, the road towards the future can be opened in many directions. Either we surrender to the state of hypnosis, which our medieval history put us into, and regress even more until we become as if we were dead and we are destroyed, or we immerse ourselves into other people's civilizations without any sanction or discipline. The latter is the choice of the alienated and the westernized who are overtaken. If we follow them, we turn away from our natural state and the foreign civilization intensifies its effect on our regression. We would be receptacles of foreign civilization with its harmfulness and disregard because we would not have any resistance or reaction to what we receive. We would either live absent from written history, as if we were asleep like the People of the Cave (who had an excuse for their sleep, contrary to us) and we would flow with the situation and different stages like a dry leaf that is carried here and there by the wind and circulated around people's paths, or we would open up to our self-essence and unite with our identity removing the dust off our resistance and reviving what is hidden within our spirits. Only then would our awareness be awakened, our conscience be cleared and our spirits renewed. In this way, our lives can be liberated; for the elements of our beings, when warmed by self-awareness, can be enflamed with a vitality and revival and we can resume our ability to move towards that which is paved for us and inherent in our heritage. The caravan can resume the journey and the wheel can turn in its orbit sailing in the Name of Allah along its course to its conclusion.[100]

Our qualification for constructing a civilization and our nomination to lead the future of humanity is a legitimate matter. It is a predetermined matter according to all standards and according to what our nation has achieved in the past, the glory of our ancestors' accomplishments, and according to the actual cultural and civil richness which time could not erase in spite of the successive achievements which followed our sunset. There are countless displays, material and spiritual, of the Muslim civilization which is still alive and obvious to our eyes.

---

[100] Ibid.

There are still those who refer to this civilization and acknowledge its values which are clear, open and successive.[101]

What distinguishes Islam is the fact that it gave humanity a creed that many legislators can look at for guidance and be indebted to it for every new legislation.[102] Islam created the civilization that carried its spiritual and intellectual characteristics and the traces of its beauty with all of its praiseworthy ethics and values. Islam's effect was widespread, contrary to other religions which established local civilizations such as in India and China.

The Roman civilization embraced the Christian creed and added to it its liberal and epicurean aspects. It changed its global message and transformed it to a creed of darkness which is destructive to man and which stands between man and his Lord.[103] It called for isolation, asceticism and escaping reality such as in the saying, "Leave what is for Allah to Allah and what is for Caesar to Caesar." The Roman transformed Christianity to the religion of monasteries, which contrary to Islam, suffers from the status quo rather than changing it.

Look at the daily lifestyle which Islam offers by observing Muslim minorities who migrated to the West. They have a noticeable presence not only because of how they practice congregational prayer on Fridays but in the way they handle their daily affairs and observe their special occasions and in the way they think. Observing them allows you to realize the open dimension that characterizes this religion; for Islam always exerts an influence and attracts people by its principles.

Indeed, the Islam which Gülen knows is the creed which is prepared to be the source for all people. It is inherently suitable for reform in all places and at all times. One of its natural characteristics is that, "It can enter the narrowest passages in an individual and in family life as well as in the social, economic, political and cultural life. It covers all of life's aspects in a way suitable for each era with a practical methodology that is more realistic."[104]

---

[101] Ibid.

[102] Ibid., pp. 49–61; especially p. 55.

[103] We mean the reformation that followed it.

[104] Gülen, *Wa Nahnu Nabni Hadaratina* (As We Are Building Our Civilization), p. 56.

This is why we yearn to establish that same civilization today which can stem from the awakening of Muslims and the feelings of their enlightened ones and their prominent intellectuals; for indeed Islam can always offer successful solutions to save humanity from today's deterioration and distortion just as it did in the past.

The Jurisprudence of Civilization

Gülen argues that faith, time and goals are the strategic cornerstones for the construction of civilization. These three aspects consider humanism in their formula; for we can reread the statement as: the human being, the faithful, the goal-oriented, and the user of time as the one who can build a civilization.

The emphasis on these three aspects for building a civilization can be found in many writings of intellectuals and philosophers. The closest to Gülen's thought is the worldview of the intellectual Malek Bennabi. He too puts conditions for the renaissance to happen: space, time and the human being.

We can read Gülen's perspective on the essential participants of building a civilization as: Allah, the universe and the human being. Gülen argues that faith is an original essence in the universe and the spirit of faith is hardwired in existence in the form of a call that flows within all realms. They all echo the meanings of these manifestations: Allah, the universe and the human being. It is the chanting praise that Allah originated all things—the whole universe with determined renewal and continuation. That call is the innate nature inherent in every being and is centralized within the veins of the creature.

The cyclic seasons, for example, are a living embodiment of the innate instinct for renewal and transformation which Allah created the creatures with. The rule of reproduction and the love of one gender to its opposite gender in all species is another manifestation of the innate instinct for formation which Allah prepared the universe with and sealed it in the living entities which live in it. It is the physical and spiritual prayer witnessed by the hearts of the enlightened ones. It participates in the fabric of his rhythm; for in reality the souls of the enlightened are like instruments issuing melodies of Divine remembrance (*dhikr*) and expressing gratitude just as the beautiful melodies of the flute express the musician's sentiments.

The main humanitarian aspect that is firmly established in Islam is one of the most known motives that cause Muslims to desire to spread its message in order to save humanity from the aggravations caused by the confusing ideologies and experimental philosophies that fall short of providing a minor level of security and tranquility.

There are many ways of preaching today, but the most effective way to spread this innate religion (*ad-din al-hanif*) to the world is when Muslims themselves become strong and build a civilization that carries the nature of Islam and reflects it spiritually and materially. When they build a role model of an Islamic-based civilization this becomes the best preaching method that will spread Islam.

The Essential Foundations of Humanism in Islam

Justice in Islam is constant. There is no doubt that Islam preserves human rights and it maintains the dignity of humanity. It proposes that no one should be distinguished from another except on the basis of God consciousness that he exhibits. Islam opens the door for everyone who embraces it to be an asset to the *ummah* with his qualifications and skills and it assures that his opinion should be considered in the affairs of the *ummah*. This is extended to include his position and responsibility towards humanity in general. Islam does not discriminate between Muslims and non-Muslims concerning human rights; for we are all Allah's people. In fact, Islam obliges the one who embraces it to be responsible towards all creatures and to be beneficial to them in accordance to the verse which states, "*You are the best nation produced (as an example) for mankind. You enjoin what is right and forbid what is wrong and believe in Allah*" (Al Imran 3:110).

It is axiomatic that the weak and belittled nation cannot be a nation of pure goodness and cannot attain the level of being qualified to enjoin what is right as known by common reason and our innate nature, as long as it stays in this state. The verse obliges us to emerge and it charges us with the duty that demands us to be strong in order to be able to carry our responsibility to prevent exploitation.

The God consciousness which Allah set as the standard measure of proximity to and distance from Him is the active spirit for people. It causes us to feel tranquil when we are in the center of ethical reliability, spiritual self-control and have a sound heart that is able to reign over lower whims and desires and to stop the ego from transgressing. In this sense, the God consciousness is the humane trait that enables the servant to attain the rank of accountability and excellent benevolence. He attains a stage in which all people praise him for his rank and his humanity as they experience his overflowing goodness and tenderness.

Such are the essential foundations for humanity which distinguish Islam and nominate it to be the religion suitable for all eras. No one can criticize the Islamic concepts and its humanity except one who is prejudiced or biased. The only reason that prevents the opponents of Islam from opening a dialogue about Islam is their fear that their fake merchant would be exposed in the debate.

Gülen makes the Islamic call comprehensive which means it should not only be gaining acknowledgment or offering services but he sees that all efforts of individuals, the collective society, and official and civic groups must join together. Nonetheless, all these efforts are still in the embryonic stage and lack experience and resources which may cause them to stop. In fact, in many cases these efforts do not cross the level of boasting, hiding shortcomings and violating Allah's rights and the ummah's rights. At this level the call cannot accomplish its goal and cannot affect a response until it is done within a comprehensive renaissance in which all Muslims participate. This renaissance puts its expectations on spreading a civilized Islamic model. The current ethical and social deterioration in the contemporary materialistic culture is waiting for this ideal model as people wait for the rising of dawn after long darkness.

The Sources of Glory and the Spiritual Dimension

Gülen's perspective of the desired civilization does not only consider the material preparation. On the contrary, he focuses on the spiritual and emotional aspects which he sees as the important foundation to achieve the renaissance.

Every year we spend a huge amount of money on purchases under the claim of taking off, but all that we spend goes in vain. This is because we are still children and we became mesmerized by the wealth we got from oil and we were hypnotized by the deception of capitalism on which we relied for consultation and expertise in preparation and learning and in all other fields.

It is obvious that a carpenter, for example, would not like to leave his job for another; otherwise the door of his provision would be shut. Similarly, if one works in the industrial profession he would not like to give its secrets to others so he can keep the value of his expertise which is the source of his livelihood. There is no doubt that as we open up to other nations and because of our naivety in interacting with the global society due to the long period of deterioration and regression, we are easily convinced and deceived and feel happy for the lower fortune of fake acceptance which leads to the continuation of our naivety and heedlessness which distinguishes us today.

In his vision, Gülen focuses on the spiritual dimension and makes the material dimension join it and follow it. When the social leaders are charged spiritually with faith, the goal becomes so clear to them that it directs their efforts towards the material preparation by selecting which tools and resources to borrow from others temporarily and which to invent and manage internally.

Gülen observed closely how some nations had developed industrially but they are now deteriorating. Their possessions, fleets, scientists, artists, researchers and professionals have become a heritage distributed among other nations like cheap merchandise that no one values.

This happened because these industrial nations ungratefully abandoned the spirit and believed that man was a mere entity controlled by conditioned actions. He follows what he is told to do and he does not follow what he is told not to, according to the authority. These nations cared only for material power and to them this has a priority over the soul. They counted on the future based on instigating conquests and supplying their fuel by exploiting the workers and taking advantage of their struggle to earn their livelihood. They kept moving with time, building renaissances and erecting edifices without the intervention of fate; for they do not believe in fate nor do they believe in the unseen or in religion. They believed that "religion is the people's opium." They did not benefit from their industrial or material surpluses at all because Allah's Will took them by surprise. These nations were shaken, ruined and split apart right in front of the world's eyes.

Gülen can read the status quo of the universe which is a characteristic the faithful believers take pride in. It is Allah's Law that dictates the ruin of the arrogant when they transgress the line set by Allah. Nobody can transgress the limits set by Allah such as one's life span, which cannot be delayed or advanced.

Gülen insists on putting the spiritual aspect on the highest pedestal for man and for the entire society and civilization. Faith is like the cement which cannot be ruined by earthquakes or storms. Faith refines the soul with sincerity and fills the heart with love.

The signs of practical faith lie deep in the believer's core being, *"Who believe in the Unseen, are steadfast in Prayer, and spend out of what We have provided for them"* (al-Baqarah 2:3). This is why the faithful believer visualizes the firm edifice of civilization and how it should be constructed. He knows the foundations on which it should be built and the tools to be used to complete it. They are faith in pure goodness, responsibility and excellent benevolence, reaching far and relying on Allah's favors Who gives man sustenance and makes him His vicegerent.

We can say that most of Mr. Gülen's books can be categorized as constructive books and we see today how the servants are applying his guidance. His book about the Prophet's biography (*as-sirah*), his book about the ascent (*as-suluk*),[105] his book about balancing measures and many of his other books explain his perspective on the spirituality of the practicing Muslim.

Gülen affirms that Islam encourages Muslims to build a civilized culture that relies on spiritual foundations that allow the heavenly eth-

---

[105] Gülen, *At-Tilal az-Zumrudiyya* (Emerald Hills of the Heart: Key Concepts in the Practice of Sufism).

ics to flow within their arteries. This civilization refines the dignity of humanity and protects man from becoming a slave to his body.

Liberating the Human Being in Islam

The concept of liberating the human being in Islam not only means saving humanity from slavery, but it also means protecting man from every situation in which he may be degraded or led to that which innate feelings and intuition cannot endure. For example, the prohibition of adultery in Islam is a protection for women who could often be exploited, abused or forced into prostitution. Under the call for personal freedom, a materialistic culture legalizes prostitution and allows advertising for it all around the world. The same argument can be applied to intoxicating beverages that people become addicted to. An addicted person is stripped of reality and enslaved to illness which the whole society should be held responsible for; for giving him the license to drink intoxicating beverages. The Prophet said, "Every intoxicating beverage is prohibited,"[106] and it is prohibited for the Muslim to sell it or give it to others. Other illnesses we can mention here are gambling, monopolies, and bribery.

Every year, the material culture wastes countless products in order to keep the prices high. The material world has a monopoly over manufacturing medicines in the cheapest places and yet most of the poor countries cannot pay their prices. The corporation's monopoly makes them cheap and sells them at high prices to augment its profits.

For this reason and many other reasons, Gülen sees that the desired civilization which is based on the Islamic renaissance would work tirelessly to treat these illnesses and eliminate these evils; for from the Islamic perspective they contradict the innate nature of the human being and they are stripping man of his humanity. The innate nature of the human being is prepared to accept that which is good and pure. Evil and oppression are not part of his innate nature. It is the responsibility of the human being to train himself to discern what is good and to ascend to his lofty rank by which Allah particularly honored him with.

---

[106] Reported by *Sahih al-Bukhari*, 4343 and by *Sahih Muslim*, 1733.

Evil is an aberrant transgression excused by a philosophy that stems from unethical, or more accurately irreligious thinking that is void of the spirit of mercy and sharing. This philosophy led to the abrogation of heavenly guidance and submitting to man-made rules, and to a man who is in opposition to Divinity and is unjustly denying the spiritual and unseen laws.

The Characteristics of the Islamic Civilization Model

Today, the Muslims' test is how to establish an original Islamic civilization model. The characteristics of this model and its spiritual, legislative and ethical constituents are outlined in the Qur'an and the enlightening guidance of the Sunnah and manifested in the excellence, originality and skillfulness of the intellectual leaders and reformers of the *ummah*.

In Gülen's opinion, the *ummah* must continue to exert the same efforts that our predecessors exerted. The *ummah* must work tirelessly to rectify the harmful effects which have ensued not only due to its long slumber but also due to the pollution that afflicted it from the materialistic culture of our era, especially when it comes to its spirituality. The ills of materialism have ruined the most important spiritual characteristics which Islam planted within us and which were handed to us centuries ago from the leaders of the worlds and their guides before our innate nature was covered up due to our deviation from our Qur'anic foundation and from the guidance of our noble Prophet.

The desired effort needed today is to rectify what was corrupted and to return to the elements of our pure religion. We must restore our spiritual assets which we let go of because of our heedlessness. We were deceived by the ornaments of the contemporary disabled culture which lost the spirit and went astray in clear confusion.

The philosophies that are based on materialism put us under their control and we have surrendered for too long to their authority. "The Qur'an prohibits us from living under others' control."[107] We have lost the essential element of strength and without it we cannot raise

---

[107] Gülen, *Wa Nahnu Nabni Hadaratina* (As We Are Building Our Civilization), p. 15.

our flag high. When we followed the most sacred, enlightening and guiding Book we were strong, and when we abandoned that Book and took it superficially we lost our strength.

Renewing our spirituality in accordance to the principles of the Qur'an and the teaching of the Sunnah can prepare us for revival, for giving, for excellent creativity and for building. In this framework we have no other way but to return to Islam which shelters us and protects us from invasions. "Islam is like the mother's milk. It has an essential role in developing our immunity and protecting us."[108] "The excellence of Islam is due to its ability to unite happiness for humanity and Divine Contentment."[109]

The second goal of our efforts must be in learning the contemporary sciences, especially the technological and experimental sciences. We must get used to thinking, to searching and to exploring. In this way, we can energize our lethargic faculties and our atrophied potentials and revive them to their original nature and vitality as they were in the past when we were the leaders of civilizations.

What we are suffering from today of regression and what pressures us and makes us feel humiliation and inferiority can be used as motivation to restore our status and energize our spirits.

Scientific methodology and the knowledge that can qualify us to build a civilization must integrate the two aspects of the intellectual and the spiritual, the intuitive and the rational, feeling and logic. This can help us overcome the deteriorating situation because the current culture has led us into illusion, fantasy, ingratitude, self-conceit and having confidence in materialism. All of that led us to a dead end. The failure of materialism in the face of life's challenges and historical transformation has shown its incapacity for evaluating and visualizing the right path to the future. "Materialism, which is the contemporary culture, has led us to a path that believes only in sensual perception with no account of having faith in Allah and submitting to His guidance and

---

[108] Ibid., p. 98.
[109] Ibid., p. 99.

taking into account the spiritual dimension which makes Allah's Will present in every pursuit."[110]

The current civilization has departed from the spiritual field and gone too far, stepping on the original ethical values under the claim of progressive thinking and personal freedom. It intentionally followed the policy of opposing everything prohibited in religions and everything rejected by our innate nature such as promiscuous public behavior. This violated all ethics and spread adultery and perverted behaviors which destroy the constituents of existence and disintegrates the family unit. This entailed the major consequences which all religions warned of. It was a matter of time before we would experience the fate determined by Allah to put a limit to the illnesses that we see today spreading around the world and warning us of such indulgences. Such is Allah's Way on earth and you cannot find a substitute to His Way.

The modes of Divine punishment are various and suitable for the extent of the crime. Divine punishment gradually intensifies until it reaches a horrifying extent. For example, we all saw the horror of the tsunami which was a reminder for all the nations to humble themselves. Nonetheless, they often return to their heedlessness and indulge in their slumber and loss. This is because of the absence of the spirituality within their hearts.

Actors and Vanguards: The Spiritual and the Intellectual Leaders

Gülen sees that man is the most prominent actor and the most important tool and cornerstone in the construction of civilization. This is why he emphasizes forming him to be a powerful and guided actor who is certain that whatever effort he exerts is an expression of gratitude which man should not forget but he should rather praise His Lord, the Giver of existence, and the Bestower of gifts.

In the absence of a guided political regime that focuses on the development of man, the society must hand this role to the elites. The *ummah* must not feel despair; for the Divine Care will always provide

---

[110] Ibid.

it with pious spiritual leaders who can awaken people's consciences and guide them.

Whenever life is darkened, Allah sends to His people a guiding light to illuminate the night and a voice that chants hope. The hardships that occur to nations demand the emergence of an opposing resistant that can confront the nightmare. Nations are like individuals; they exhibit power and emerge strong when a hardship, which is beyond what they can bear, strikes. It is as if external power were given to them to support them in the time of danger and to repulse the evil away.

Surely, the appeal of goodness is what makes their ears return to listen to the voices of the pious who call them to be steadfast and stand firm in the face of the breaking storm.

The emergence of every unequaled pious person is like the breaking of dawn after darkness or like the emergence of fresh water in the desert. The unequaled, who are prepared by destiny to be the makers of history and the builders of civilization, appear at times of intense darkness and overwhelming afflictions. This is because at such times, no one can devote himself and give his soul except those who have mighty spirits, the possessors of determination, and the heirs of the Prophets.

Their appearance at the time of hardship and in the midst of darkness is in accordance to the law of balance which Allah continues life with. It is Allah's determined term. The pursuit of these great spiritual and intellectual leaders is a manifestation of the Divine law in the universe which states that, "There is no disease that Allah has sent down, except that He also has sent down its treatment."

Those leaders become a flame that is always kindled and their efforts reach far and they become the niches within which are lamps. Then they become a station of light that illuminates the whole land. Then they become like a star or a sun illuminating the horizon and attracting people: "*He brings the living out of the dead*" (al-An'am 6:95). This is the case of the pious in their nations. They emerge out of the depths of darkness with a humanitarian fabric which others were stripped of and threw it away. They stand in the midst of falsehood with the weapon of faith. They are unique in their spiritual stations.

They are rejected and pushed away and cannot find any empathy or friend as if they were standing against the truth and not the supporters of the truth and the callers for nobility. Ordinary weak people watch them struggle against the power of falsehood and they do not support them. Under the propaganda of the proponents of falsehood ordinary people start to become hostile towards those who are trying to defend their rights and protect them.

The possessors of determination feel immense sorrow that causes their hearts to bleed, seeing all these arrows thrown at them from all directions. They do not hesitate to confront falsehood and refute its arguments. They stand firm in the battle and they do not escape the confrontation.

Those devout leaders are in the midst of fire. However, out of their persistence, resistance is born, weak in the beginning like a seed in the womb of the earth. Only a few realize that they can persist in spite of being attacked from all directions. The certainty of victory within the hearts of the people of faith increases slowly but gradually until the sprouts open and the spring comes. But how do the reformers prepare for that future and how do they visualize it and how do they pave the way for it? It is by continuous burning that warmness is created and life flows. Out of a single egg, a bird emerges then another, then another until a flock of birds emerges. Then, the torch becomes a flame reaching heaven, attracting attention from across the world.

When the immunization of faith is injected within the souls of the youth, mercy dwells within their hearts and they grow up in love and love becomes the manner that colors their personalities and shapes their beings as long as they live. The fermentation of goodness grows because the souls' desires become refined and pursue only that which is virtuous. This is because of the immunization of love which was injected within them and which allows the readiness for perfection. Their souls would naturally be repulsed by evil and wrongdoings and by everything that violates virtue and opposes the spiritual nature.

This is the guidance that assures spiritual provision which starts to move through circles and on platforms, and between groups and in written materials that can reach larger circles. It outlines a luminous line on the horizon making a high standard for all seekers and pious followers who pursue a virtuous life.

The spiritual leaders are the engineers of humanity's perfection. They realize that the refinement of man is not an easy task and that it can take one's whole life. The need for construction is immense and the spiritual provision must be quickly supplied in the right dose. This is why spiritual leaders rely on teaching self-discipline. They realize that when the noble soul is attracted to the forums of righteousness it can quickly earn vitality. The soul thrives by its fortune of enlightenment and goes to where it should go as its roots are deeply within the soil. This soul can supply itself with vitality like a jungle tree that naturally grows providing shadow for its surroundings and allowing new sprouts to emerge to take its place when it grows old.

Every gathering the pious forms is transformed to a generator that produces light. Each student of the school of faith gains from the alchemy of love and the nutrition of growth that assures him to be able to continue his journey and gradually ascend in the orbits of refinement. This strengthens the soul even more and transforms the student's life in his surrounding ocean of life and clarifies to him in which way he can serve and give. His spiritual connection with the past eras of glory deepens and he lives in an atmosphere of unity at all times as if he were one of the great Companions of the era of glory. He takes his provision from the springs of Muhammad, peace and blessings be upon him, as if he were the one who directly taught him. Indeed, Muhammad ibn Abdullah is the best of all creatures, the guided teacher and the leader of humanity.[111]

When we water the youth with fresh faith we put him on the road towards building a true civilization. This is because the faithful is strong in the face of invasions and he is protected from the pollution that life is filled with. Instead of joining the norm of corrupted people who are the outcome of society's heedless attitudes about virtues, he becomes the agent of purification and cleansing. Purity overwhelms his very essence and he becomes the carrier of goodness, excellence and benev-

---

[111] Ibid., pp. 13–17.

olence. He first pours these virtues on his surroundings, his family and those who interact with him. The noble element that is polished by religious discipline is one of the agents of goodness, peace, and tranquility. After he grows from the stage of straightening, volunteering and discipline he becomes an element of the reform. He spends his life working silently in continuous devotion resembling the devotion of angels. We have seen examples like a type of diamond among the servants.

Some of them carry the duty of forming a family unit based on discipline and spiritual reform. He raises his children following good ethics, magnanimity and spreading that which is worthy of praise. From these children, a chain of offspring emerges carrying the same values and lofty ethics. In this way the circle of virtues and beauty keep expanding and the sprouts of goodness spread horizontally and grow vertically increasing the areas of enlightenment and prosperity and making the land of social reality green. Thus, generation after generation can follow the path towards spiritual maturity and virtuous civility. This is naturally followed by strengthening creativity and productivity which propagates originality in all fields of life which results in the emergence of the unique cultural model that is qualified for leadership and global mastery.[112]

Indeed, a civilization can be original and deep if it follows this doctrine which is based on gradual growth that can expand its space to all fields. When the roots of civilization are planted, its growth can take place quickly. With time, it breaks its slow rhythm and defeats regression which may initially slow its progress, but eventually it flows easily and quickly. The value of originality is that it can radiate and cover the full horizon and so it becomes the pursuit of all people.

Originality means that people preserve their culture and that citizens naturally grow with its excellence. This supplies their souls with the dynamic energy that can produce its own creative solutions and its own abundance. Thus, every student in the school that is qualified to teach and discipline is a blessed seed that can produce seven stalks

---

[112] Ibid.

and within each stalk there would be one hundred seeds. This augments the assets upon which the virtuous city can be born.

Motivations and Incentives

The material goal has an obvious motive. Its aim is the desired end and the tool of reward and recompense. Its ability to motivate is immediate and it gathers people. Nonetheless, this is subject to diminishment and so it needs continuous renewal and stimulation which must be sensual and knowledgeable.

As for the non-materialistic motive, it depends on spiritual rewards and success is measured by one's ethical values; for actualizing the ideal virtues is the noblest concept and it should be the real pursuit of those who are spiritual.

Spiritual struggles are void of material gains. If any material gain is found it is usually second in importance. If spiritual struggles are what reveal the true essence of the person, then it is what distinguishes the possessors of steadfastness and masterful wills from ordinary people.

The individual who is only moved by material motives always remains exposed to failure whenever his way of earning these gains is obstructed and he then usually rushes in search of a substitute. On the contrary, the one who is motivated by spiritual motives does not hesitate to pay an offering even if it were his very soul. He gives his life to his pursuit; for the value of his life depends on the value of the ideal virtues. He glorifies that which is loftier than matter and more precious than perishable materials. Thus, his life, the most valuable thing he owns, is something he does not hesitate to give for the sake of preserving the ideal values.

By living principles, the spirit lives. If the person is martyred for the sake of his values, he is promised an eternal life. On the other hand, the one who battles in order to gain material goods gains them abstractedly from their ideal dimension and his value is only equal to the perishable goods. This is the nature of consumerism and each possession passes away. Consumption is accidental not essential. Gold itself can melt in fire to its basic elements in spite of its value. In this sense, we must realize that any material gain is subject to loss and such degeneration and corruption does not touch any spiritual aspect at all.

This noble consideration is inherent within the core of the human being; for it is the essential essence of his existence and he receives that intuitively and from life itself. The contemporary culture with its atheist philosophy presents every ethical tendency as an inferior trait in man. There is no doubt that man is weak but the Creator, Glory to Him, prepared him for purification and made ethics and virtues as motivators that raise man to perfection.

Because our primitive physical nature is low and can drag us to what could injure our sound sense due to it belonging to the animal world, Allah sent messages and Messengers to guide people. He made religion lead to beauty and goodness. No one should be forced to follow a particular religion that inures his sound taste and common sense; for the teachings of a true religion should encourage the noble qualities that are concealed as potentialities within the innate nature.

The ungrateful culture that is anti-religion continues to trivialize the value of virtues and dwarfs the soul on account of glorifying the physical and the materialistic. This has caused great harm to everything sacred and the flame of virtues have diminished and even extinguished the fire that lit the conscience of man. It insulted everything noble and stepped on all that is worthy of praise. Other aspects were praised and have replaced the ancient values. This was motivated by selfishness and enslavement to materialism.

The material motive became the mover of the wills through the widely spread ideology of physical and materialistic competition and not confronting Satan as the law of transformation and development. This caused regression in the sense of accountability and deafened the consciences; for it tied it to numbers and quantities and the ratio of salaries in the battle of deception verses living. This is why Gülen argues for the obligation of confronting this foolish flow which is almost turning life upside down and taking it out of its natural course.

The Essential Foundations of Gülen's Civil Perspective

One of the most important aspects, upon which Gülen forms his civil perspective, is the revival of the spirit of the true religion and saturating the civil sectors with the spiritual values to free contemporary life of all diseases and blemishes.

Legends are an important element of European and Western sentiments and one of the most prominent aspects of the essence of its literature which was inspired by Greek and Roman cultures. The West still employs these legends in its epistemology and establishes the foundations of its ideology on them. There is no doubt then that religion is the essential essence of the Islamic identity. Islam, with its valuable praiseworthy qualities and the holistic notion of its pursuits can contain the diverse cultures of all nations from which the dawn of Islam emerged or to which its light reached. Islam rid these nations of all aspects of polytheism and aimed to integrate its noble elements with each culture. In this way it integrated a common identity and all Muslims carry these characteristics.

Islam, with all of its rites and rituals is the powerful motivation for the soul and the sentiments and feelings of the Muslim. It also is the cause of action and construction. Rituals are the essential guide that is present in all states.[113]

The importance of religion is that it is a continuous energy and renewing power that does not fall into profanity contrary to the other ideologies as we explained before. Thus, religion always has the ability to revive the ashes from within. Religion has the ability to line people up and to move them to achieve major goals and to meet crucial challenges.

People revolt against tyranny and are certain that they would be victorious even though they have nothing except their faith; for faith is the weapon that is unparalleled and upon which victory is determined. Islam is a daily worship that guides one's behavior. It is the incubator of values and the natural material within which all ethics grow in its diverse images and colors.

---

[113] Ibid., p. 58.

The culture in Islamic communities is closely related to religion and it even affects the atheist's behavior that lives in this culture. This is because religion is agreeable to the innate nature of the human being and it is not separated from it. The mark which Islam leaves upon those whom it touches cannot be erased even if the human being tries to uproot it from the depth of his being.

The personality of man and the collective personality of the society are shaped by culture, which is the first school of education and the vast space that can be built by discipline. Thus, cultural reform aims at educating the generations by kindling its own spiritual energy and manifesting its sacred elements. Religion should not be used as a tool to achieve a particular goal and then be abandoned. Such a relationship with religion would be very weak, fake, hypocritical, opportunistic and biased. This relationship is made by ideologies that are promoted by heedless adherents. But because reality prevails, sooner or later the edifices of conjecture fall right before the watchers' eyes and all their dreams totter.

Culture is enriched and opens at times when the hearts are charged with faith. The faithful individual who is sincere in his faith and the group that is true to its creed and the society that has more pious people, is a culture that is colored by creed. The heart that is inhabited by God consciousness overflows with love and straightforwardness and is dynamic and energized and races to goodness. Culture is like plasma within which the cells of faith are produced. Creed provides the culture with its values and its energy and so the culture is weakened by weakened values[114] and is strengthened by the strength of its values.

All calls of reform shyly rely on the spiritual values within the individuals and the groups. These values stem from religion and seek to create a cultural field to strengthen the motive for goodness, which religion aims at. "Indeed, culture with all of its diverse colors in the reforming society circulates in the circumference of belief and it drinks from the spring of beliefs, feeding on its nutrition. Culture grows with

---

[114] This means that culture is straightened by the straightness of the ethical curve it follows and is made crooked by its crookedness.

belief and is transformed by it from one state to another that transcends place and time."[115]

Through cultural motivation, China mobilized its lines, leading its people through high mountains, and crooked hills which they scraped by their nails and paved by their hands. Beliefs led nations to fight against Hitler. Communism fought with blood in its confusion, believing it was saving man from the narrow gate of ideologies to an earthly paradise. Nonetheless, this type of mobilizing culture can make nations dizzy for a period of time but it does not continue forever because new generations come with new thoughts and take the *ummah* into successive stages one eliminating another. But religion in its essence is prepared to continue; for it depends on its mobilizing power, on the loftiest ethics which come from the Creator, glory to His Majesty.

Certainly, all ideologies claim to defend ethics in order to reach their pursuits. In other words, it covers its goals with a sophistical deception that makes it hard to have true insight into its plot and so people become confused.

The Central Role of Religion in the Reform

Religion is the most important factor in motivating people. It is the most powerful dynamic tool that mobilizes people and the most effective means to spread ethics and civil behavior. This is because in the fold of religion, individuals and societies realize their equality. They share the same responsibilities and expect the same reward and punishment. This makes all people stand equal distance from the One Creator and leads to their realization that they share common obligations which are not dictated by one of them, but they are obliged to follow the guidance that transcends humanity. The path is not illustrated by a person; for even the calls of the reformers and the preachers are no more than a reminder of what the creed itself dictates. In this sense, the reformers and the preachers only alert people to what they are heedless of and point to where they have deviated from the Divine law.

---

[115] Gülen, *Wa Nahnu Nabni Hadaratina* (As We Are Building Our Civilization), p. 79.

By turning on the religious engine within the souls, we can originate a social culture which produces modest social behavior in conformity with the Divine law as much as possible. This allows the society to resume its spiritual vitality and its balanced manner as it returns to its original culture. Witnessing corruption hurts man and he is offended by anything that violates the essential principles of the Divine law and ethics.

The desired cultural base is to guarantee the society its self-protection from all destructive beliefs and foreign ideologies through training the spirit in cultural unity and augmenting its sensitivity and its ability to react suitably towards any breach or seduction that may pollute the matrix of values or that may try to make it deviate from its nature and its path.[116]

The dynamics of protection and positive conservation of the original culture enables it to exchange with and have positive dialogues with other cultures. The reformers' efforts form a limited circle of reform in a small range. Nonetheless, this circle has the capacity to attract people with its originality which carries the luminous light of the sacred principles that it embodies. This enables their small circle to expand. The nobility of its principles has a preferential influence on people and the ability to guide. The reform circle becomes like a lighthouse that turns attention to itself.

By the innate religion we can guarantee that our civilization is supported with a purified spirit. By ethical-based education we can revive the souls from being unconscious of spiritual and material issues. When a culture emerges from the core of religion it prepares the society to heal its spiritual illness. It is a type of self-healing that is guided by an enlightened cultural atmosphere that can dissolve all distortions.

The difference between secular immunization which Gülen calls for and that of a liberal philosophy is that he walks the society on a pedagogical path by which the society itself can recognize its illnesses and the sources of these illnesses and can willingly seek the treatment and correct the crookedness of its path. This can happen when the soci-

---

[116] Ibid., p. 22.

ety becomes conscious of what may cause harm to the society and senses when its creed is violated.[117]

Certainly, life would not be void of distortions in spite of all efforts of reform. Nonetheless, the reformed life is like a healthy body which remains in a self-perfecting mode, ridding itself from its disease. This is the nature of life itself. Evil cannot be eliminated from life but evil should not continue to be the norm.

Liberalism opened the door towards a bestial future for humanity where anomalies become the norms. It prevented the human being from expressing his feelings towards these anomalies and forced him to bless them; for otherwise he would be called "backward" or "fundamentalist" or "old-fashioned."[118]

It is a must to integrate knowledge of history with religious and cultural motives for the desired revival to occur. Society will have put its feet in the right direction and be determined to follow it to protect itself from emptiness if the society becomes knowledgeable of its past and studies the stages which caused the *ummah* to be alienated from that past and understands the characteristics of the stages of strength and the stages of weakness as well as comprehends the *ummah*'s gains and the causes of victory and defeat on its path.

In emphasizing the importance of knowing history, Gülen does not hesitate to look at the pre-Islamic eras, reminding people of the primitive Turkish culture and how it was far from civilization. In studying history in its entirety, Gülen gives the generations a full picture with all of its dimensions. This prepares the generations to recognize what Turkey gained by belonging to Islam. Islam made Turkey the leader of the world for many centuries after it was only mere tribes who were fighting each other for their livelihood and who could only herd sheep.

---

[117] Ibid., p. 33.

[118] The word "fundamentalist" became one of the worst curses and one of the worst accusations that political, secular and Western ethics can accuse someone of being. Unfortunately, we started to imitate that trend and use the same vocabulary. The word "old fashioned" means ancient and decayed.

Islam accomplished the same thing for the Arabs, the Barbers and many other nations. It mobilized them after they were lethargic and made them the leaders of the world for many centuries.

According to Gülen, history is one of the most important driving forces that can mobilize the social, the ethical and the cultural components to act. Thus, it is inescapable to invest in teaching history to qualify the *ummah* to pave its road and to correct the path of misery and alienation.

Looking at the features of the past can reveal the collective identity and reflect both its beauty and its distortions in the mirror of history. The relationship of Islam and history is proportional and concomitant. Most of the Islamic nations lost interest in their pre-Islamic history. This is because by living in Islam, these nations were able to write history in gold. Even the nations who had past glory felt ashamed of the distortions, the corruption and the primitivism of its past creeds before they embraced Islam and its sun shined on them.

History lessons should have priority in the education of the people in order to rescue them from the confusing alienation and from the deviation of the road they are taking and realize that they were exposed to intended obliteration of their cultural history from the collective memory and to the distortion of the historical realities of their past. It is a relentless effort to cut people off from their roots and make them live as orphans without past support in order to restrict them to becoming a tail of someone else's secular body and culture.

Framework and Leadership

To make and project success regardless of its kind, there must be leaders who look after it, manage the operation and follow the stages of execution. This is because advancing the work and guaranteeing its accuracy and success demands an observing eye, a vigilant mind, a hand of a craftsman and the management of a wise leader who can find resources for the budget required to finish the plan and complete the project. It is well-known that successful programs have to be carried out by experts, facilitators, and hard workers who are involved in doing the work.

Designing a project and managing it requires determination and subtleties upon which the fate of the project relies, the framework of the project is a very important point which Gülen emphasizes and recommends. He not only looked at designing and facilitation as a technical activity that should be performed in the ordinary way as any other work, but he also looked at it as the core of spiritual effort and a characteristic of worship which can assure that the project is completed in the best way possible. This is because work is not a duty that man must perform but it is a form of worship by which man comes closer to His Lord and a form of purification by which his feelings are refined and he can gain more meaning in life. Every achievement is a step on the ascending ladder. In this way, performance itself becomes the achievement which raises the performer to a distinguished state. The performer becomes like an artist with flowing feelings, and a sensitive touch. He is Sufi (i.e. pure) with spiritual tastes and a luminous vision.

In the inner being of the faithful believer, who often brings himself to accountability, there is deep love and sweetness that makes any action he performs come out with a very unique nature because in its reality it is the echo of his love and a trace of his sweetness which his soul is satiated with. This confers excellence, beauty and acceptance on anything he does, even if he hands you a cup of water it would be very satisfying to you.

Without doubt, Gülen's own life helped him set full and effective measurements concerning the characteristics of the leaders who can become responsible for the execution of the plans and the projects. He was raised and passed many stages in his life managing his own affairs which took extraordinary turns.

Gülen's Origin and Its Influence

Gülen grew up searching and joining the centers of education that were not available for others in similar situations to his. He traveled from one area to another in his pursuit of knowledge. He lived in a continuous state of readiness and alertness. He led a lonely life and took care of himself and that required him to be focused and to learn how to manage any situation whether it was related to his public life or to his personal affairs. He did not neglect any of his duties and obligations; for he always realized that his spiritual retreat and study required him to extend his awakening to the rest of his surroundings and relationships to assure the continuation of the path. He passed one stage after the other and that increased his travels from one place to another, which enriched his experience, augmented his persistence and his ability to pierce through the hidden aspects of the life of man and of the unknown.

Gülen set the measurements of leadership and the framework of managing major projects from his own path in life, from his experiences, from his spiritual enlightenment, and from his intellectual epiphanies. During his youth, he moderated the gatherings of the knights and school camps. He was responsible for managing their budgets. Out of donated money, he would buy the food and emergency kits and prepare accommodation and transportation. He would provide a safe and joyful atmosphere for the students and the participants. He would make these camps and gatherings like open windows for real life. He would emphasize good education and discipline. In this way, he gained experience in managing money and in doing business. He also gained the ability to harmonize different groups of youth. This gave him the expertise of leadership and wise management. Added to this was the speaking ability he gained by serving as the Imam of the mosque. All of these experiences clarified the meanings of professional performance that qualified him as a guide and allowed him to observe how his colleagues perform their jobs in the mosques or in other fields.

Certainly, Gülen's celibacy contributed to his success as an administrator and manager. In his life, he learnt how to manage both of his major and minor affairs and how to set his priorities straight. From his biography we learnt that even in winter he used to perform ablution for the dawn prayer using such cold water that it was almost frozen in the pipes. He would pour water on himself in a place that was opened to such extreme cold that even rocks would moan from it.

This shows us the type of man he is. His religious duties are his first priority and he protects them more than he protects his own soul even though Islam makes protecting the soul equivalent to protecting religion, except in cases where one has to give his own soul for the sake of his faith. There is no doubt then, that one who lived connected to his Lord to this degree of devotion is an excellent spiritual being. Sweetness is the apparent sign of that type of devotion. Thus, whoever chooses devotion to be his lifestyle would attain the ideal rank which qualifies him to do righteous work and prepares him to serve.

Sweetness not only comes from one's devotion to performing acts of worship, even though it is the core source of the revered ones, but sweetness is shown in embodying the essential goals of faith which is to help people and communities to walk towards the safe shore and to guide them and serve them to bring out the best in them and allow them to advance in their way to attain Divine Pleasure.

The Effect of Relinquishing and Beautification on Gülen

A sign of sincerity is when a devoted one's heart is enraptured by a unique penetrating love that no other can compete with him for it. The sweetness of the pious ones stems from the way which they relinquish and follow as an essential aspect to mobilize their efforts and liberate themselves.

The blessing of relinquishing facilitates the way the seeker widens the horizon of his spiritual contemplation of life and of people's states. Spiritual retreats enable the seeker to bring to his consciousness the spirit of the role models and to walk in accordance to the doctrine of the Prophets, especially Prophet Muhammad, peace and blessings be upon him. The seeker can then acquire the qualities of mercy, sympathy, compassion and caring for all creatures. This type of pursuit is the right pursuit which brings humanity to its lofty spiritual and material levels. Thus, the spiritual retreat is the cornerstone upon which the seekers strive to bring themselves to Divine proximity. In this sense, spiritual retreats do not mean mere seclusion, asceticism and being distant from people and events. Spiritual retreats can rather become a continuous state within the heart which is full of Divine remembrance, prayers and glorification which can be transformed in the physical reality as knowledge and qualification that enables the seeker to raise the spiritual awareness in the society and transform their psychological and social status. He can help people who fulfill their duties for the sake of Allah's Love. In this sense, their vision of this world and the next are integrated so that they can enjoy peace and tranquility. They are satisfied only by praising and glorifying Allah in return for all that they do.

How could one who takes the Messenger of Allah as his role model, his leader, his inspirer and guide not be a brilliant leader, organizer and manager?

There is sweetness in being in retreat at all times and in all places whether the servant is in his prayer corner in his own house or whether he is walking in the markets looking for solutions to improve people's states. In both cases, the servant is connected with his Lord and is always in His Presence. He learned to live partly conscious of his daily life with people but also conscious of his Lord with his whole heart and thoughts. Even if he sometimes becomes unaware, he would soon reject this heedlessness and work hard to compensate for this loss. He is his own self-watcher and this is why all of his work is blessed. Thus, the seeker always strives to attain what their guides, the Prophets and Messengers attained because they are the role models.

They feel that time is passing them by like clouds pass. So they are always alert and if they have control over things they would soar across the horizons, racing time to achieve what they dream of.

The Reformers and the Permanence of Burning the Ego

In spite of their certainty that Allah has given them a great portion of His blessings they wish they could have had more time to serve Him more. They wish life and age would allow them to do more. In this way, they live, burning themselves continuously. Their shoulders are burdened by that which mountains cannot bear. They are drowned in continuous work. Their work becomes a persistent prayer. They are immersed in the intermediate realm which is the source of the essence of their work and effort. They mobilize those who are determined and they seek resources that would ensure the continuation of their constructive projects. They consider doing acts of goodness as the most important obligation for which the faithful believer lives.

To them, life is the plantation for the Hereafter and the fortunate ones are those who realize that true life is the final abode and that this life is meant for work and for construction. This is why their motto is, "We do not live to exist but we exist to live."[119]

From living alone and devoted to Allah, Gülen gained intellectual and spiritual insights which strengthened his innate intelligence, sagacity and intuition. This prepared him to manage the major projects in the way towards a renaissance that can change the status quo and prepare the ground for a liberating journey with no return.

Look how he minimizes distances and expands his efforts across the continents and offers a matrix of projects for the renaissance in which numerous numbers of workers in all fields and all levels are mobilized. His projects stun people and win their admiration as they see them grow in size, in style and in the characteristics that distinguish them.

By continuous unification, the intellectual can gain extraordinary executive abilities which stem from his reading of signs and subtleties. He lets the soul dwell in the luminous times and the good eras, starting with the era of the rising apostleship and how the Prophet's life transformed souls, changed the status quo and directed history in the opposite direction in less than twenty years. Also passing through the decades of the Rightly Guided successors (al-Khulafa ar-Rashidun) in which they fertilized the earth and ruled over two tyrannical empires, the Roman and Persian, and stretched their wings across the center of the earth, keeping many nations under the shade of the Islamic flag. By letting the soul dwell in these times and contemplate all of that, one

---

[119] Gülen, *Wa Nahnu Nabni Hadaratina* (As We Are Building Our Civilization).

can understand the secrets of that history and gain the most precious prize that a student or a researcher can get. He can comprehend the history that led to the founding of the Islamic civilization and made it take off for centuries, during which it colored the world with the vivid colors of Islam.

The clarity of the seer's insight increases by retrieving historical experiences and by comprehending the demands of the Divine law. This is because within this context, there are golden treasures of lessons and wisdom which enables it to prosper.

The leader finds another opportunity to learn in his effort to build and lead. This learning is deduced from his direct engagement with reality and his battle with challenges. This enriches his vision and makes him gain flexibility. His vision demands execution, efficacy and renewal. There is no room for errors; for whoever makes this his loftiest goal is achieving a renaissance and overcoming the deteriorated situation. To join the caravan one must not be a miser when it comes to giving of his time, talents and efforts.

The Inspired Mind and the Intellectual Leaders

Gülen sees that a renaissance is made by an inspired mind. This is because the transformation needs to be led by a visionary leader who knows how to achieve the plan. Gülen argues that the best leaders are the Prophets and in their forefront is our Prophet, Muhammad, peace and blessings be upon him. His mission was global and its goal was to guide man to eternal life. Islam clarified the path and landmarks that keep us on it. It guarantees the human being to be the vicegerent of Allah on earth. The characteristics of the leader who is qualified to lead the renaissance of civilization are essentially heart-based. His qualities and goals are Divinely provided; for Allah knows the leader's firm faith and He is the Most Powerful who has all the affairs in His hands and from Him his servant receives his guidance and guarantee of success.

Faith here is the essential element; for the faithful believer's heart is full of confidence in His Lord. Thus, he finds extraordinary energy within his spirit as the connection between him and heaven are established. By being attracted to his Lord, the ego no longer battles no matter how exhausting the service is or how much suffering the believer might endure.

The possessors of love speak of how their souls are enraptured by ecstasy, joy and a sense of bliss amidst hardship. They pass one hardship after the other as they are crushed and wounded, but their spirits are content to transcend beyond pain. This is because the heart in all of its states and situations is in the Presence, ecstatic by the reassuring breezes that blow upon them.

The Men of Service and Their Role in the Construction

We see how Gülen relies on volunteers to achieve the renaissance. Such are the servants who have submitted and are provided by strength from the atmosphere that encourages sacrifice. This atmosphere is charged by the electric current of faith which comes from their hearts that are full of the awe of Allah. They are always connected to the guides that give them responsible fatherly care. These are the purified ones who keep advancing on the way of enlightenment with an ever growing spiritual enthusiasm.

They are the disciples who waged battles against their egos and listened to their leader. *"Say: work and Allah will see your work as well as His Messenger and His faithful believers—then you will be returned to the unseen and witnessing realm so that He may foretell you what you would do"* (at-Tawbah 9:105). They too have a fortune of love.

Deep involvement and engagement with life does not increase and become fruitful until the spiritual connection of the servants becomes firm. Therefore, the servants must exert their utmost effort so that the renaissance becomes their personal existence and the hope for the future for which all sacrifices become worthy.

In his description of the servants and their role in the construction Gülen says, "Our renewed revival of our culture requires men who are eager to have faith, and intellectual engineers who are touring the future with their intellectual vision. It needs geniuses who embrace existence and events with their artistic voices, exploring with their sensitivities and subtle examinations the new horizons that are beyond the horizon we are in."[120]

Gülen emphasizes the qualities that these servants should have, "The troops of consciousness must perform functions such as opening new horizons before our systematic closed thinking. They must renew our desensitized evaluating faculty which has turned far from heaven, by making it circulate within the Qur'anic orbit. In this way, they will not become heedless of the secret that connects man with all creatures and with life. They must exemplify a religious model which embodies the religious teachings and actualizes them attentively. In addition, they must observe one of the most important rules of navigating the path to Allah, which is to be in harmony with the possessor of the Divine law and to be forgiving, easy and harmonizing. Their very trait should be giving glad-tidings not repulsing others. They must end the chronic sterility that has existed for too long by using the power of knowledge and contemplation of the Islamic rules to interpret it for people. They must transform every school or temple, every street or house, to observatories detecting the truth which is concealed beyond this existence, this life and man. They must activate the visionary windows, which have been on hold for centuries, and contemplate the infinite. In their agendas, Islam must take priority and be integrated with all aspects of life. They must have the sensitivity to evaluate the causes and effects in accordance to an ascending relationship. They must act based on rationality. These are the ones who can help us renew our lives and teach us reliance on the Eternal Existing Presence."[121]

Without doubt, Gülen's perspective aims at the ideal stage which the servants should attain for the sake of reviving the *ummah*. Certainly, he conferred high standards and ranks on the servants which demands of them to acquire certain qualities, attitudes, and a willingness to sacrifice, which he himself has gradually acquired in the life of giving that he leads.

---

[120] Ibid., p. 34.
[121] Ibid., p. 20.

We can find him looking for the birth of these companions that are determined to make this succeed. He realizes that the vanguards whom Allah ordained to follow his flag will have offspring that can advance the goal and carry the responsibility of seizing a triumph by which the souls attain happiness. "We are a nation watching and waiting for resolute men who have a will and can exert great effort in carrying this responsibility. We are not in need of charity and intellectual systems that beg from external or internal sources. We are in urgent need of the physicians of the soul and the intellect who can evoke within people a sense of responsibility and concern. We are in need of the physicians' wisdom which will allow us to go deep within our own souls instead of into all the false promises of fleeting happiness. They can at once lift us to levels from which we can see the beginning and the end joined together."[122]

The servant must be beautified by the trait of deep love because the one who is deeply engaged in life must be aware of all the subtle courageous missions. No one can be charged with continuous exhausting missions except one who is persistent and who is able to live the Hereafter in this life.

The way to the renaissance cannot afford to lose the effort of anyone. A wall can be built with some broken bricks and upside down bricks and also by stones and can be put together with gypsum and clay.

Nonetheless, subtle missions, decision making and conquests require submitters who are attracted to ascend and who dance in ecstasy in the midst of hardships when the fire is intensified. "These are the ones who attain the level of distinction. None can compete with them due to their mighty hearts. They also do not compete with anyone because they are enraptured by the visions of Divine Pleasure."[123]

"Divine selection places the enraptured people in the forefront and looks with reservation at the religious ones or those who appear to be religious. The religious ones are usually overtaken by selfishness which prevents them from attaining full self-emptiness that sanctifies

---

[122] Ibid., p. 89.
[123] Ibid.

them from opportunism. Their harm is worse than the non-religious ones even though both of them do not revere religion and do not allow free-thinking. Both of them are closed-minded when it comes to sharing and diversifying."[124] Thus, both of them are obstacles in the way of achieving harmony along the way.

The Strategy of Integrating Science and Religion

One of the foundations of reviving the *ummah*'s consciousness is spreading a sense of responsibility among all citizens and explaining to them that the project of renaissance is the essence of the Divine Mandate and the duty of every individual. What causes weakness in most of the projects and even causes them to stop is the fragmentation of the *ummah* where one group or party adopts the project and does not open it up to the whole nation on all levels. These projects are destined to remain small, isolated and even fail.

In the West, competition for power is based on the desire to raise the condition of the whole country and maintain it in order to be in the forefront. This is contrary to the political conflicts in our countries which depend on influencing groups which seek to monopolize power and authority. They function like the mafia.

The renaissance must be the goal of all the diverse groups of the *ummah*. The incapacity to lead and mobilize the whole nation causes the projects to fail because the hands are not joined and the efforts are not united.

The mission of the enlightened faithful vanguards requires them to be able to mobilize all energies and supporters from all social classes. The responsibility of reaching the grassroots and strengthening its base is the responsibility of the enlightened, the foremost in the way of the renaissance.

There is no doubt that what threatens the serious programs and actually causes them to be ruined and end is if they are represented to people as a sectarian project that may not interest the whole society but only interests those who serve it. When people feel they are just

124 Ibid., p. 47.

an audience they object to the project, obstruct it and may cause it to become bankrupt because of the desire to compete for leadership which can cause the project to weaken and to fail.

The renaissance is not on a schedule to execute it and then be lax and enjoy the harvest of its fruits, but rather it is a transformation that includes all members of the society considering their behavior, education and aspirations. It makes righteous actions become the norm that constitute life, the purpose by which one exists, the ethics by which all unite and the essence without which there would not be being, or honor, or dignity.

This is why the vanguards have to carry the torch and become the flame itself. They consume themselves in expanding the areas in which people can contribute, so much so that no effort is missed but all efforts should be attracted to and directed to empower the caravan.

Indeed, the best way to attract people and expand the circle of workers is the exemplary behavior of the individuals and groups of leaders. Showing tolerance, generosity and humbleness demands all workers be strong and exemplary.

The creation of the culture of unity, sharing, team work and common ground is one of the prominent purposes of education which Gülen stresses. All the constituents of work and interactions in Islam are based on the principles of unity and productivity. Islam cares for a collective and fruitful aim; for it was established on the principle of community. Thus, Islam is a religion of projects and the continuous renewal of renaissances. It prepares people for positive and constructive work and to be immersed in major transformations. This continuation stems from Divine Support that has power over everything.

Overcoming the Gaps among Methodology, Performance and Initiatives

Gülen emphasizes that harmony is the cornerstone of the renaissance and so no weakness should affect that essential principle and cause what Gülen calls "gaps." To have a good plan every program should have all the essential components that it needs and there should be ways to cover any lack in any field. If the program does not have these integrated components, the result will fall short or will exceed its limits or it may be in vain because if it does not respond to a certain need it will be useless.

It is shocking to see many of the educational systems in the Arab world fruitless and without aim. There are thousands of youth who graduate from many universities, institutions and high schools without having a national plan to use them, not only to overcome unemployment, but also because education should serve a better role concerning providing manpower for the real job market in all fields. Thus, the machine produces graduates and they go to waste and their efforts go to waste. They should rather work to expand the nations' industries, agriculture, chemical and atomic research and services. Education should encourage creativity to allow the graduates to compete and reach international markets with their exported products.

Many mechanics graduate from Islamic and Arab universities but our countries still import cars and machines, even nails and screwdrivers. This is because the schools' curriculums are not well thought out and designed. They only prepare our graduates to be candidates for forced emigration. They end up benefiting others while we paid the cost of their education. This is because national planning did not take into account the creation of jobs which can advance the society and transform it from importing almost everything to being self-sufficient and even an exporter. In this way, our countries continue to squander their wealth by acting randomly without having an engineer to guide them or the intelligence to rectify their paths and put them on the road to prosperity.

Gülen stresses the importance of harmony to avoid gaps on the performance level. He firmly believes that the renaissance requires collective effort, yet it also encourages individual initiatives and supports the initiators. In fact, in the project of renaissance, these individuals must be sought and taken on. Gülen likes to integrate all individual initiatives in the fabric of the plan. In this way, it would not be random, its efforts would not be futile or go out of the context of the matrix of unity or turn out to be opposed to what the plan aimed for.

By lining up and integrating all individual efforts and single initiatives, the program of the renaissance becomes systematic and organized. In this sense, growth becomes collective and complete and the ability of natural expansion or parallel expansion or successive expansion becomes possible and inevitable.

"Indeed, if all efforts and individual initiatives are not executed within the context of a collective movement and are not organized well, it would lead to conflicts between individuals and between different branches. This will eventually lead to chaos."[125]

Having a working schedule and distributing the load of work is the healthy dynamic that can prepare more opportunities and open new horizons from the service offered. The concept of organizing and harmonizing all programs of the development and all units and branches enable all of them to expand and multiply. Gülen also stresses detecting unique talents and on finding suitable positions for them to strengthen the push for the future. Those who excel can originate a moving force under the condition of working in the context of the collective project and in harmony with it. "The flames of individual uniqueness should never be turned off but they should be cared for so that not an atom's weight of energy would be squandered, but be directed to achieve the desired goal."[126]

Order, discipline and planning cannot prevail except in an atmosphere of tolerance and inclusiveness of all groups and factions that offer the service. Any malfunction in these relationships can certainly cause malfunction of the projects and cause harm.

Gülen lives with the spirit of unity; for even when he is absent from the circles he still lives with the intimate friends he brings into his heart. He speaks with them in the way of the devotees, "...and devote yourself to Him with (complete) devotion" (al-Muzzammil 73:8).

Gülen believes there are great blessings (barakah) in being in a community which is naturally provided with self-purification in an atmosphere of brotherhood. There are blessings in belonging to a commu-

---

[125] Ibid, p. 44.
[126] Ibid.

nity where everyone feels the favor of others and that he is nothing without this unity and without seeing his reflection in his coworkers.

Therefore, self-discipline, being flexible, submitting to the community's demand, avoiding conflicts, harmonizing perspectives and subduing selfishness are some of the commandments which Gülen set for all workers. The servant should not forget that he is following the guidance of longing and love even in the midst of immersing himself in details. Detachment should be the servant's essential quality. Otherwise, he would be easily provoked and a mere trainee. He must continue to exert more pure effort to attain the threshold of the radiating Light. The servant must have acumen and must be quick in comprehending every useful provision that the community exhibits. This is one of the core duties of the servant.

Contemporary culture offers ideas and tools for construction from which we can select and integrate with our doctrine and rectify them to suit the spirit of servitude. Acumen and awakening can leave the door open for enhancement and creativity while refining the unified efforts. This can make servitude a path that attracts youth from all directions and who have diverse talents and can add to the services different roles and advance them. Renaissance means continuous refinement and an ascent of ethics and civilization. History is like a book where the youth compete to write its story. They devote their lives and work to write it. Nonetheless, all servants must put their faith in Allah as the sole measure of success in all the work they do and in all the goals they aim for.